RAND NATIONAL DEFENSE RESEARCH INSTITUTE

T0290506

Officer Career Management

Steps Toward Modernization in the 2018 and 2019 National Defense Authorization Acts

Albert A. Robbert, Katherine L. Kidder, Caitlin Lee,
Agnes Gereben Schaefer, William H. Waggy

Prepared for the Office of the Secretary of Defense

For more information on this publication, visit www.rand.org/t/RR2875

Library of Congress Cataloging-in-Publication Data is available for this publication.
ISBN: 978-1-9774-0237-0

Published by the RAND Corporation, Santa Monica, Calif.
© Copyright 2019 RAND Corporation
RAND® is a registered trademark.

*Cover: U.S. Marine Corps photo by Lance Cpl. David McKenzie,
2nd MARDIV, Combat Camera.*

Support RAND
Make a tax-deductible charitable contribution at
www.rand.org/giving/contribute

www.rand.org

Preface

Section 572 of the National Defense Authorization Act (NDAA) for fiscal year (FY) 2018 (Pub. L. 115-91) called for the Secretary of Defense, in consultation with the secretaries of the military departments, to provide two reports on policies for regular and reserve officer career management. The reports are intended to provide perspectives on the body of statutory provisions commonly referred to as the Defense Officer Personnel Management Act (DOPMA) and the Reserve Officer Personnel Management Act (ROPMA). The first report addressed the sequencing of promotion lists. The second report encompassed 15 additional promotion or career management issues. Sections 501 through 507 of the NDAA for FY 2018 (Pub. L. 115-232) enacted some of the provisions explored in the 2018 reporting requirements and required further reporting on a new promotion-related flexibility.

The director of Officer and Enlisted Personnel Management within the Office of the Secretary of Defense asked the RAND National Defense Research Institute for assistance in obtaining perspectives from service secretariat, military, and reserve staffs on the issues to be covered in the various reports required by the 2018 legislation, organizing the perspectives, and providing additional information or analysis helpful in informing potential statutory or policy changes. This report summarizes that work and also outlines related statutory changes introduced in the 2019 legislation. The work was completed during calendar year 2018.

This research was sponsored by the Office of the Secretary of Defense and conducted within the Forces and Resources Policy Center of the RAND Corporation's National Defense Research Institute, a federally funded research and development center sponsored by the Office of the Secretary of Defense, the Joint Staff, the Unified Combatant Commands, the Navy, the Marine Corps, the defense agencies, and the defense Intelligence Community.

For more information on the RAND Forces and Resources Policy Center, see www.rand.org/nsrd/ndri/centers/frp or contact the director (contact information is provided on the webpage).

Contents

Figures

Tables

Summary

Section 572 of the National Defense Authorization Act (NDAA) for fiscal year (FY) 2018 (Pub. L. 115-91) required the Secretary of Defense, in consultation with the secretaries of the military departments, to provide two reports to the Senate and House Armed Services Committees on policies for regular and reserve officer career management. These reports pertained to prospective changes in the body of statutory provisions commonly referred to as the Defense Officer Personnel Management Act (DOPMA) and the Reserve Officer Personnel Management Act (ROPMA). The first report covered promotion list sequencing, and the second addressed an additional 15 elements of review specified in the NDAA. The RAND Corporation's National Defense Research Institute assisted in the preparation of those reports. The present report provides the material developed by the institute for the reports to the Armed Services Committees. The work was completed during calendar year 2018.

Methodology

The primary methods used in assembling this report were literature reviews and interviews with current policymakers—principals and other representatives from the service secretariats and military staffs responsible for officer management policy.[1] RAND and similar research organizations have periodically assessed various aspects of DOPMA and ROPMA. We reviewed these assessments to identify key issues that would serve as a foundation for interviews with current policymakers in the military services.

We organized our service interviews, and this report, by grouping the 16 required reporting topics into five bins: promotions, tenure, talent management, active/reserve component permeability, and crosscutting issues. Many of the reporting topics could easily fit in more than one of these bins; we divided them in a way that we thought

---

[1] Due to the volume of reporting requirements, most interviews were conducted with action officers responsible for policy development, but they also included one deputy chief of staff, several deputy assistant secretaries, and other general officers or senior executive service members. The organizational level of interviewees varied by military department, at the department's discretion.

would facilitate interviewing service representatives and analyzing their responses. The topic areas are shown in Appendix A.

Promotions

The reporting topics relating primarily to promotions are

- evaluation of the impact on officer retention of granting promotion boards the authority to recommend officers of particular merit be placed at the top of the promotion list
- an analysis of the reasons and frequency with which officers in the grade of O-3 or above are passed over for promotion to the next-highest grade, particularly those officers who have pursued advanced degrees, broadening assignments, and nontraditional career paths
- an analysis of the utility and feasibility of creating new competitive categories or an independent career and promotion path for officers in low-density military occupational specialties
- an analysis of how the armed forces can avoid an officer corps disproportionately weighted toward officers serving in the grades of major, lieutenant colonel, and colonel and Navy grades of lieutenant commander, commander, and captain, if statutory officer grade caps are relaxed.

What We Found

While there is some room for added flexibility in the promotion system, service representatives indicated that, by and large, DOPMA/ROPMA promotion structures still work well. While the service representatives were supportive of additional legislative flexibilities to manage their promotion processes, they were very cautious about implementation for fear of creating stagnation in a closed promotion system that they believe currently flows well.

The military services widely support legislative reform to provide service secretaries with the authority to sequence all or part of their promotion lists on the basis of merit. But the services also want to exercise their own discretion regarding how they use this authority.

The service representatives did identify the need for some minor adjustments to accommodate the recruitment and retention of two types of officers in particular. First, they agreed that it was reasonable to amend DOPMA/ROPMA to accommodate officers who gain additional education or career-broadening experience that would increase their value to the force. One option would be to allow those officers to opt out of promotion consideration.[2] A second option would be to deem them "fully quali-fied" on condition of completing stipulated career milestones after promoting to the next rank.

Second, the service representatives widely agreed that there was a need to better accommodate officers in emerging mission areas, such as cyber operations special-ists. In light of this concern, they supported options to develop technical tracks that provide alternatives to traditional promotion patterns and to offer constructive credit for advanced education or experience gained before commissioning.[3] However, some service representatives recognized that constructive credit will have limited appeal in attracting highly experienced accessions because it is not used in basic pay determina-tions (10 U.S.C. 533). In all cases, however, the service representatives emphasized the need for service secretary discretion to implement these flexibilities in a controlled and judicious manner.

Tenure

The reporting topics relating primarily to tenure are

- a statistical analysis based on exit surveys and other data available to the military departments on the impact that current personnel policies under DOPMA have on recruiting and retention of qualified regular and reserve officers of the armed forces; specifically, the statistical analysis shall include an estimate of the number of officers who leave the armed forces each year because of dissatisfaction with the current personnel policies, including career progression, promotion policies, and a perceived lack of opportunity for schooling and broadening assignments
- an analysis of the benefits and limitations of the current promotion time lines and the "up-or-out" system required by policy and law
- an analysis of the utility and feasibility of encouraging officers to pursue careers of lengths that vary from the traditional 20-year military career and the mecha-nisms that could be employed to encourage officers to pursue these varying career lengths
- an analysis of the current officer force–shaping authorities and any changes needed to these authorities to improve recruiting, retention, and readiness

---

[2]   That option is now available to service secretaries based on Section 501 of the FY 2019 NDAA.

[3]   The opt-out and alternative promotion authority provisions contained in the FY 2019 NDAA provide means for developing promotion policies suitable for a technical track. The FY 2019 NDAA also included an amend-ment to DOPMA/ROPMA that would allow for the services to award more constructive credit. See Sections 502, 505, and 507 of the FY 2019 NDAA, discussed in Chapter Seven.

- an analysis of any other matters the Secretary of Defense considers appropriate to improve the effective recruitment and retention of officers.

What We Found

Consistent with our findings on other topics, the service representatives agreed that, with respect to tenure management, DOPMA/ROPMA provides a solid foundation for officer career management. While the service representatives were open to increased flexibility, they maintained that the fundamental nature of the statutory up-or-out system is effective.

Where the services are pursuing tenure flexibilities, two themes emerge. First, while increased flexibilities are desirable, the service representatives still prefer a high threshold for executing any new authority or flexibility: approval at the service secretary level. Second, representatives from each of the services articulated that flexibilities should be exercised based on the needs of the service and must be tied to requirements. While the increase in tenure flexibilities may provide retention incentives and increase individuals' career satisfaction, the goal of the flexibilities is to meet the needs of the service—not simply to meet individual desires.

The service representatives maintained that DOPMA was initially created as the solution to a problem: promotion stagnation for junior officers. As such, the services are cognizant that any reforms or efforts to modernize DOPMA must not invalidate the gains DOPMA has brought to officer personnel management since 1980.

Talent Management

The reporting topics relating primarily to talent management are

- an analysis of the extent to which current personnel policies inhibit the professional development of officers
- an analysis of the efficacy of officer talent management systems currently used by the military departments
- an analysis of how best to encourage and facilitate the recruitment and retention of officers with technical expertise.

What We Found

The services have devised standardized career paths that effectively develop tactically proficient leaders.[4] Those career paths account for facets of DOPMA and ROPMA

---

[4] We use the term *tactical* in this context as relating to the immediate employment of military forces, particularly at a smaller unit level, as opposed to *strategic*, which relates to long-term or broader organizational or operational considerations.

that constrain professional development models, such as cohort management and the up-or-out system. Standardized career progression may place a burden on career fields that require additional training. Relaxing those constraints can change professional development models as currently employed, such as by allowing additional time for training-intensive career fields.

While there is general satisfaction with most of DOPMA's and ROPMA's professional development implications, changes to DOPMA and ROPMA could change the relationship between the development of tactical expertise and the development of strategic expertise. There is some indication that tactical expertise crowds out the development of strategic expertise, especially early in a military career. As Army representatives mentioned, changes to a promotion board's culture could change professional development models.

The services have wide latitude in talent management, and that latitude manifests in alternative approaches to the definition of talent. While the concept of talent evolves in some circumstances, the services rely on requirements to drive talent management. To some extent, broadening is a career luxury, as operational requirements are prioritized ahead of broadening.

Technical expertise applies to an ever-changing compendium of skills, but insights gained from a current focus on acquisition and retention of cyber expertise can apply to other emerging areas. The services representatives see changes to constructive credit as an important recruitment tool.

Active/Reserve Component Permeability

One topic pertained to active/reserve component permeability: the utility and feasibility of allowing officers to transition between active duty and reserve active status repeatedly and seamlessly throughout the course of their military careers.

What We Found

The service representatives we spoke with agree that there are benefits to permeability—including the potential to recruit and retain individuals who are seeking more flexible career paths. However, representatives from the services also identified several barriers to permeability, including cultural, legal, and policy barriers. The current scrolling process is one of the biggest barriers. In considering options for improving it, there seems to be support for appointment to a service instead of a component, avoiding the delays incurred in rescrolling an officer moving from one component to another within the same service. There is also support for merging the active-duty list and reserve active-status list, as long as the services retain flexibility to use competitive categories to consider regular and reserve officers for promotion separately.

Crosscutting Topics

Three topics applied broadly across all of the bins:

- an analysis of what actions have been or could be taken within current statutory authority to address officer management challenges
- an analysis of what actions can be taken by the armed forces to change the institutional culture regarding commonly held perceptions on appropriate promotion time lines, career progression, and traditional career paths
- an analysis of the impact that increased flexibility in promotion, assignments, and career length would have on officer competency in their military occupational specialties.

What We Found

The services currently use multiple competitive categories, selective continuation, and personalized talent management systems to greater or lesser degrees. Services less invested in these approaches are considering increasing usage of them.

Service cultures have thoroughly internalized the regularity of DOPMA/ROPMA promotion structures and the selectivity shaped by grade ceilings, up-or-out provisions, and grade-specific tenure limits. Management of core warfighting occupations and many support occupations is so well calibrated to these structures that service representatives have difficulty contemplating alternatives to them. While the inflexibility of the system has its critics, service leadership and individual officers have varying degrees of discomfort in moving away from it. Where substantive career management changes are contemplated, they are generally to address niche issues in highly technical functions or those that require extensive education or experience out of mainstream service functions. Changes to this culture are likely to evolve slowly as the services gain experience with new flexibilities in the niches where they are introduced.

2019 National Defense Authorization Act Changes

The 2019 NDAA contained several statutory changes that are closely related to many of the exploratory reporting requirements contained in the 2018 NDAA. These changes

- remove a previous age restriction at time of commissioning
- allow for additional constructive service credit at commissioning
- standardize temporary promotion authority across military departments
- allow resequencing of promotion lists based on merit
- allow officers to opt out of promotion consideration under some circumstances
- allow selective consideration of more junior officers

- provide an alternative promotion framework for officers in designated competitive categories.

Conclusions and Recommendations

We reached several broad conclusions:

- The military departments believe that DOPMA and ROPMA continue to provide an effective overall framework for managing the careers of officers in core warfighting communities.
- Where change is needed, it is primarily to accommodate needs in low-density occupations, to foster the pursuit of unconventional but useful career paths, or to permit an earlier shift of more promising officers from tactical to strategic skill development.
- The services are more open now to new flexibilities in officer career management than they were when Secretary of Defense Ashton Carter's Force of the Future proposals were first unveiled.
- The one phenomenon that signals a need for new flexibilities more than any other is the employment of military personnel in offensive cyber warfare. There is a perception, not yet fully in focus, that conventional career management approaches may not yield the human capital needed for success in this mission set.

Openness of service representatives to new officer career management flexibilities is married to a strong sense that implementation should be at the discretion of service secretaries. We sense a growing willingness to differentiate career and talent management approaches across the services and for different needs within each of the services, but with secretarial discretion that allows the services to tailor their approaches to specific needs and to allow gradual adoption of new flexibilities as their longer-range consequences become better understood.

Our recommendation to the services is to search for innovative ways to take advantage of existing and emerging flexibilities. Our recommendation to legislators is to provide service secretaries with the latitude to adapt innovatively to their current and future challenges.

Abbreviations

ACS	advanced civilian schools
ADL	active-duty list
AGR	active Guard reserve
ANG	Air National Guard
APZ	above the zone
ARNG	Army National Guard
BPZ	below the zone
BRS	Blended Retirement System
DoD	Department of Defense
DoDI	Department of Defense Instruction
DOPMA	Defense Officer Personnel Management Act
eSERB	enhanced selective early retirement board
FAO	foreign area officer
FY	fiscal year
IPZ	in the zone
KSAO	knowledge, skills, abilities, and other attributes
MOS	military occupational specialty
NDAA	National Defense Authorization Act
RASL	reserve active-status list
ROPMA	Reserve Officer Personnel Management Act
ROTC	Reserve Officers' Training Corps
SERB	selective early retirement board
SOFS-A	Status of Forces Survey of Active-Duty Members
SOFS-R	Status of Forces Survey of Reserve Component Members
STEM	science, technology, engineering, or mathematics
U.S.C.	United States Code

CHAPTER ONE

Introduction

Section 572 of the National Defense Authorization Act (NDAA) for fiscal year (FY) 2018 (Pub. L. 115-91) required the Secretary of Defense, in consultation with the secretaries of the military departments, to provide two reports on policies for regular and reserve officer career management. The reports cover 16 enumerated elements pertaining to officer promotion and career management, many but not all of which are regulated by portions of Title 10 of the United States Code (U.S.C.), commonly referred to as the Defense Officer Personnel Management Act (DOPMA) and the Reserve Officer Personnel Management Act (ROPMA). The first report covered promotion list sequencing, and the second addressed the additional 15 elements of review specified in the NDAA. The RAND Corporation's National Defense Research Institute assisted in the preparation of those reports. A full list of the elements is in Appendix A. The present report contains the material developed by the institute for both reports provided by the Department of Defense (DoD) to the Armed Services Committees. The work was completed during calendar year 2018.

This report provides information of interest to legislators, legislative staffs, and defense and service officials contemplating changes in officer promotion policy. It captures the perspectives of the military departments and services regarding potential statutory or DoD policy changes and how service practices might be modified as a result.

Background

DOPMA, enacted in 1980 as Public Law 96-513, modified or changed substantial portions of Title 10 pertaining to active officer personnel management. ROPMA, enacted in 1994 as part of the NDAA for FY 1995 (Pub. L. 103-337), changed similar portions of Title 10 pertaining to reserve officers. Since their enactment, the provisions of these laws have been subject to continuing analysis, review, and revision, but their major features have remained intact. These include (Parcell and Kraus, 2010)

- a closed system in which, with few exceptions, officers enter at low grades and higher grades are filled through internal promotion
- a pyramidal structure for the field grades (O-4 through O-6) relative to each other and to the company grades (O-1 through O-3) collectively, formed by grade ceiling tables based on total officer strength in each of the services
- a competitive, up-or-out career flow maintained by established high years of tenure for various grades and requirements that officers twice nonselected for promotion are subject to involuntary separation
- seniority-based promotion timing, including time-in-grade requirements for promotion, defined zones of promotion consideration based on date of rank, and promotion lists sequenced by date of rank
- uniformity across services, with statutory provisions authorizing or directing the Secretary of Defense to prescribe uniform regulations for implementation.

Methodology

The primary methods used in assembling this report were literature reviews and interviews with current policymakers—principals and other representatives from the service secretariats and military staffs responsible for officer management policy.[1] RAND and similar research organizations have periodically assessed various aspects of DOPMA and ROPMA. We reviewed these assessments to identify key issues that would serve as a foundation for interviews with current policymakers in the military services.

To aid in conducting interviews and presenting results, we arrayed the 16 elements raised in the 2018 NDAA in five bins: promotions, tenure, talent management, active/reserve permeability, and crosscutting issues. The bins are shown in Appendix A. Many of the reporting topics could easily fit in more than one of these bins; we divided them in a way that we thought would facilitate interviewing service representatives and analyzing their responses. While binning the topics was done for methodological reasons, we recognize that DOPMA/ROPMA policies are tightly integrated and that a change to a promotion policy might, for example, also affect tenure or talent management considerations.

Yardley et al. (2005, p. 2) mapped some of these relationships as shown in Figure 1.1. Beginning at the bottom right corner of the map, service end strength (1), entry qualifications (3a), and constructive credit (3b) affect the number, characteristics, and entry grade of new officers. Officers are placed on an active duty list (4), which estab-

---

[1]   Due to the volume of reporting requirements, most interviews were conducted with action officers responsible for policy development, but they also included one deputy chief of staff, several deputy assistant secretaries, and other general officers or senior executive service members. Organizational levels of interviewees varied by military department, at the department's discretion.

Figure 1.1
Concept Map of Active Component Officer Career Management

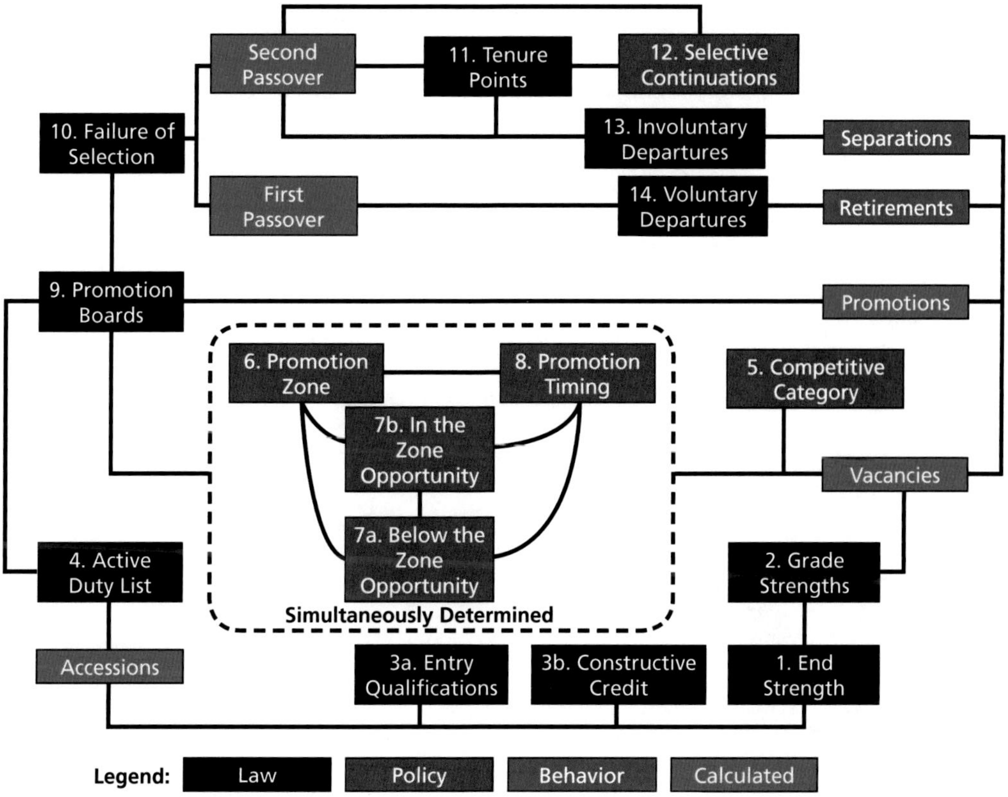

SOURCE: Yardley et al., 2005.

lishes officers' seniority and is used in construction of promotion zones. Promotion timing (8) and opportunity (7a, 7b) are driven more by policy than by law and are mainly functions of how promotion zones (6) are constructed. Competitive categories (5) are set by service policy. The selections for promotion are made by promotion boards (9) whose functions are prescribed by law, although with direction from the service secretaries. The law defines those who were in a promotion zone but not selected for promotion as having failed of selection (10), and those who twice fail in a grade face mandatory tenure points (11) set by law. Officers may face involuntary departures (13) if they are not selectively continued (12), or officers may depart the service voluntarily (14). Both result in vacancies, which are the difference between officer inventory and grade strengths (2). Vacancies at most grades are filled by promotion, although O-1s and some officers in higher grades enter via accessions.

Organization of the Report

Chapters Two through Six, corresponding to the five bins mentioned earlier, provide findings from our interviews and analyses related to the 16 reporting requirements from the FY 2018 NDAA. Chapter Seven contains flexibilities introduced in the FY 2019 NDAA in response to the analyses provided by DoD in its report to Congress. Chapter Eight provides our conclusions and recommendations.

CHAPTER TWO

Promotions

This chapter provides insight into the services' views of the need for DOPMA/ROPMA modernization related to officer promotions. It examines how the services would reconcile two competing tensions within the promotion system codified in DOPMA/ROPMA. On one hand, the services are interested in preserving seniority-based promotion timing, codified in DOPMA/ROPMA, which ensures that officers continue moving through the system. Officers are promoted in accordance with time-in-grade requirements and defined zones of promotion consideration based on date of rank. On the other hand, there is a growing view among the services that seniority-based promotion timing tends to be less accommodating to officers pursuing nontraditional career paths, who might need additional time to hit specific career milestones or to develop a particular set of skills.

This tension between keeping the personnel system flowing and allowing for nontraditional paths is a central theme in the four FY 2018 NDAA reporting requirements related to promotions. The four requirements are as follows:

- evaluation of the impact on officer retention of granting promotion boards the authority to recommend officers of particular merit be placed at the top of the promotion list
- an analysis of the reasons and frequency with which officers in the grade of O-3 or above are passed over for promotion to the next-highest grade, particularly those officers who have pursued advanced degrees, broadening assignments, and nontraditional career paths
- an analysis of the utility and feasibility of creating new competitive categories or an independent career and promotion path for officers in low-density military occupational specialties (MOSs)
- an analysis of how the armed forces can avoid an officer corps disproportionately weighted toward officers serving in the grades of major, lieutenant colonel, and colonel and Navy grades of lieutenant commander, commander, and captain, if statutory officer grade caps are relaxed.

The first reporting requirement asks about a method to accelerate the advancement of certain officers identified as being of higher merit. The second asks whether the seniority-based promotion timing outlined in DOPMA/ROPMA is hurting DoD's ability to access and retain officers on nontraditional paths. The third inquires as to whether more flexibilities, such as new competitive categories, new promotion paths, or an option to "opt out" of the promotion process, are needed to accommodate these officers. The last reporting requirement recognizes that if more people were allowed to step off the traditional path, by either opting out of the promotion process or entering the services laterally at a higher grade than O-1, the services might seek some relaxation of grade ceilings in order to avoid degradation in promotion opportunity or timing. It seeks clarification on how the services would temper this flexibility.

Before moving on to discuss the services' responses to each of these reporting requirements and the additional areas of interest, two additional points are in order. First, service representatives generally agree that DOPMA/ROPMA still works as a framework for ensuring the growth of a highly qualified and talented officer corps for most of their needs. Overall, representatives said they feel the current system is recruiting and retaining top-quality officers and therefore there is no need for a drastic overhaul of DOPMA/ROPMA or the military personnel system in general. Second, while all the services generally support more flexible DOPMA/ROPMA language on promotions, they want to ensure that the service secretaries can retain maximum authority to decide how far to implement reforms.

The next four sections of this chapter will discuss the service representatives' reactions to each of the four promotion-related reporting requirements and their support for related changes to DOPMA/ROPMA language related to promotions. The chapter then concludes with a summary of the services' responses to the reporting requirements.

Reporting Requirement: Evaluation of the Impact on Officer Retention of Granting Promotion Boards the Authority to Recommend Officers of Particular Merit Be Placed at the Top of the Promotion List

Technical Issues

As indicated in Chapter One, current statutory provisions produce relatively stable ranking among officers as they progress through the grade structure. The broadest principle is that rank among officers is determined by the dates of their original appointments as officers. There are, however, a number of departures from that broad principle; some occur when initial appointments are made, whereas others occur at later points. Proposed changes to the sequencing of promotion lists introduce another potential departure from the general principle. This chapter examines how non-seniority-based sequencing of promotion lists would interact with these other departures.

Original Appointments

The date of rank of an original appointment is determined by the service secretary (10 U.S.C. 741(d)(1)). DoD policy (DoD Instruction [DoDI] 1310.01) specifies that for regular officers this will be the date of the appointment, with some exceptions:

- Reserve Officers' Training Corps (ROTC) graduates appointed in May or June have the same date of rank as service academy graduates.
- Appointees with constructive service credit will have their dates of rank adjusted by the amount of service credit.[1]
- Officers transitioning from a reserve status to original appointment as a regular officer generally retain their dates of rank; in some circumstances, their dates of rank may be adjusted to reflect qualifications and experience.

For original appointment as a reserve officer with no prior commissioned service, date of rank is generally date of appointment or federal recognition. Constructive credit may be applied. Regular officers transitioning to a reserve status generally retain their grade and date of rank.

Seniority-Based Dates of Rank

Regular Officers

Under current DOPMA provisions, relative rank for regular officers changes when they are promoted below the zone (BPZ) (in which case they leap ahead of peers who are considered but not selected BPZ) or when they are nonselected in the zone (IPZ) or above the zone (APZ) considerations (in which case their relative rank falls behind those promoted in that cycle). Otherwise, regular officers selected for promotion are promoted in monthly increments, as service-wide vacancies occur, in order of their dates of rank.

Reserve Officers in the Army, Air Force, and National Guard

For Army and Air Force Reserve officers, including National Guard and Air National Guard (ANG) officers, additional considerations related to position vacancies come into play (10 U.S.C. 14308(e) and 14316). A reserve officer selected by a *mandatory* promotion board (a promotion-zone-based board, comparable to a regular officer promotion board) may be promoted out of sequence to fill a higher-graded position (i.e., a position that is authorized at a higher grade than the officer under consideration). Similarly, an officer selected by a *vacancy* promotion board (convened to consider officers nominated to fill specific position vacancies before meeting a mandatory promo-

---

[1] *Constructive credit* is an adjustment of service dates used in determining the grade and the rank of a person receiving an original appointment as a commissioned officer. Per 10 U.S.C. 533, it may be based on certain specified types of advanced education, training, or special experience.

tion board) will be promoted ahead of officers with earlier dates of rank who have not been so nominated and selected.

National Guard officers may also be selected by their states for promotion, based on position vacancies. After selection, they are considered for federal recognition and given a date of rank on the date on which federal recognition is extended. These officers must be occupying a position at or above the promote-to grade in order to be promoted.

Because considerations regarding assignment to higher-graded positions drive much of the sequencing of Army and Air Force Reserve or Guard promotions, order-of-merit sequencing would have limited application unless other legislative changes are also made. Some categories such as Army active Guard reserve (AGR) officers are promoted without higher-grade assignment constraints. If legislation is changed to provide service secretaries latitude in promotion list sequencing, it would be beneficial to also relax some higher-grade assignment requirements.

Reserve Officers in the Navy and Marine Corps

Neither the Navy nor the Marine Corps uses position vacancy considerations in its reserve officer promotion processes. Navy Reserve promotions are, in some cases, based on a running-mate system (10 U.S.C. 14306) in which the reservist is matched up with an active-duty officer to determine eligibility for promotion consideration. When so matched, a reserve officer selected for promotion assumes the new grade with the same date of rank as the running mate (10 U.S.C. 14308(d)). If the running mate is selected BPZ or is nonselected for promotion, a new running mate is identified. If legislation is changed to provide the service secretaries latitude in promotion list sequencing, the Secretary of the Navy would likely find it beneficial to use that latitude in both Navy and Marine Corps Reserve officer promotions.

Merit-Based Promotion List Sequencing

At the time our interviews were conducted, legislative proposals had been developed that would provide service secretaries the authority to sequence promotion lists, or parts thereof, on the basis of merit rather than seniority. As discussed in Chapter Seven, this flexibility was provided in the 2019 NDAA. As discussed later, the services would exercise this authority in different ways. Some services might elevate a high-merit subset of those selected by a promotion board, perhaps 15 percent of those selected, to the top of a promotion list. BPZ selectees would likely be heavily represented within the high-merit subset. However, BPZ selectees would be ranked by order of merit against IPZ and APZ selectees rather than automatically going to the top of the high-merit list; some BPZ selectees might not fall high enough on an order-of-merit list to be included in a high-merit subset. Other services might sequence the entire promotion list in order of merit, perhaps using seniority as a tiebreaker among officers in various order-of-merit ranges.

Figure 2.1
Notional Promotion Timing Within an In-the-Zone Promotion Cycle

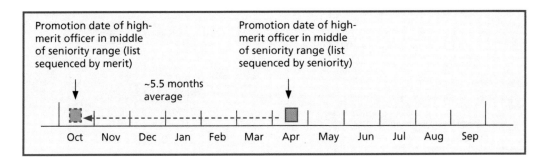

For officers selected IPZ, sequencing by order of merit would result in high-merit officers being promoted at or near the beginning of a promotion cycle rather than where they would fall by seniority within the cycle.[2] Figure 2.1 illustrates how the date of promotion for an IPZ selectee might be affected. In this notional example, the promotion cycle, defined as the period over which all officers on a specific promotion list are promoted, is bounded by a fiscal year.[3] When the promotion list is sequenced by seniority, promotion of officers selected IPZ would be spread out over most or all months of the fiscal year. But with merit-based sequencing, a high-merit officer near the middle of the seniority range among selectees who would otherwise be promoted near the middle of the promotion cycle (in April, for example) might instead be promoted the previous October. Depending on how a service phases its promotions across the promotion cycle, high-merit IPZ officers might pin on the new grade on average about 5.5 months earlier than with seniority-based sequencing.[4]

For officers selected BPZ, the promotion timing advantage would often be greater. Figure 2.2 illustrates some of the possibilities. In this figure, each horizontal line represents promotion cycles for three IPZ cohorts. We used the term *due course* here, as is common in DOPMA-related discussions, to indicate the promotion pattern for officers who are selected IPZ for every grade. The far right segments represent the promotion cycles in which an officer would be promoted if selected in due course. The

---

[2] In this context, *promoted* means actually assuming the higher grade and being paid at the higher-grade rate, after having been *selected* for promotion by a promotion board.

[3] Some services confine an annual promotion cycle for each grade to a fiscal year. Others vary the length and timing of their promotion cycles so that the span of time over which those selected by a board are promoted may be longer or shorter than a year and may start at points other than the beginning of a fiscal year—generally, the month after all promotions have been made from the previous promotion list for the same grade.

[4] The Navy would be an exception. Since the Navy phases its promotions such that two-thirds are promoted in the last month of a fiscal year, high-merit officers might gain more than a 5.5-month advantage.

Figure 2.2
Promotion Timing with Seniority- and Merit-Based Promotion List Sequencing

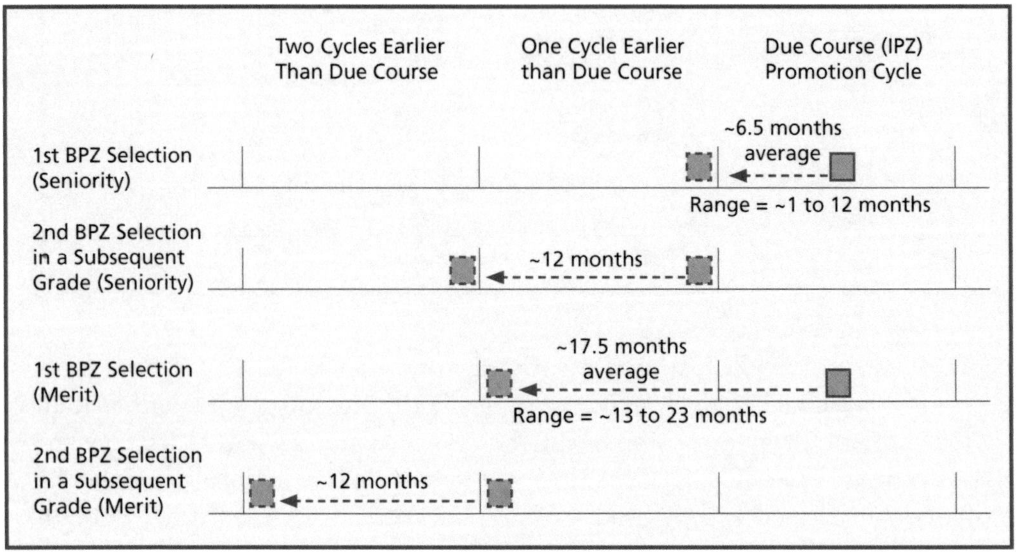

center and leftmost segments represent the two cycles preceding an officer's due-course promotion cycle.

The first line of the figure illustrates the effect of a first BPZ selection with a seniority-based promotion list sequence. With a one-year-early BPZ selection, the officer joins the cohort of more-senior officers who were selected IPZ by the same board and is promoted in the cycle preceding the one in which he or she would otherwise have been promoted in due course. However, since the BPZ selectee is junior to the IPZ selectees on the promotion list, he or she is promoted at or near the end of the promotion cycle. His or her promotion date is accelerated by anywhere from 1 to 12 months (or possibly longer in services with variable-length promotion cycles), averaging perhaps 6.5 months if he or she would have been in the middle of the seniority range if selected in due course the following year.

The second line shows the impact if the same officer is selected for a second one-year-early BPZ promotion in a subsequent grade. He or she would advance from the tail end of the cohort joined with his or her first BPZ promotion to the tail end of yet another earlier promotion cycle, resulting in an additional 12-month acceleration of his or her promotion date. He or she will have, on average, about 18 months' time in grade when due-course officers who were originally commissioned on the same date as him or her are eventually promoted to that grade.

The third and fourth lines in Figure 2.2 illustrate the typical effects of BPZ selections with merit-based promotion list sequencing. Instead of being promoted at the tail end of the cycle before the one in which they would have been selected in due course, high-merit BPZ officers would be promoted at or near the beginning of that cycle, gaining an average of about 18 months time in grade compared with their expected due-course promotion date. With another BPZ selection in a subsequent grade, they might move from the beginning of the cohort with which they were first promoted BPZ to the beginning of yet another cohort, cumulatively gaining, on average, about 30 months compared with due-course officers.

Service Processes, Perspectives, and Potential Implementation

The military services widely supported legislative reform to provide service secretaries with the authority to sequence all or part of their promotion lists on the basis of merit. But the services also want to exercise their own discretion regarding how they use this authority.

The remainder of this section on promotion sequencing examines our findings regarding merit-based reforms drawn from interviews with representatives involved in personnel policy from each of the services. We begin with a discussion of why the services each supported reforming DOPMA/ROPMA legislation to allow for merit-based promotion sequencing and why they believed service secretaries should have flexibility in implementing the reform. We then turn to a discussion of how each of the services would implement its newfound authority.

Widespread Service Support for Merit-Based Promotion Sequencing

Service representatives cited two main advantages of the merit-based system over the current, seniority-based system as mandated in existing DOPMA/ROPMA legislation. First, the services noted that merit-based promotion sequencing would generally foster a culture that rewards officers for high performance. They cited a second and related advantage regarding BPZ selectees, who are disadvantaged in the current, seniority-based system because, as explained previously, their early selection often results in a very limited gain in time in grade and an even more limited gain in extrinsic rewards (pay). Since pay is tied to time in service rather than time in grade, officers who are promoted BPZ experience only a temporary pay increase when they are promoted to a higher rank; once their due-course peers are promoted, they are all paid at the same rate again based on their grade and time in service. A merit-based promotion sequencing process would allow BPZ selectees to be more heavily represented at the top of a promotion list, lengthening the period in which their pay would exceed that of due-course officers and further reinforcing a culture that rewards high achievement.

Service representatives saw the advantages of merit-based promotion sequencing as outweighing any potential drawbacks. First, the proposal appears to be cost neutral; the services contend that it would be carried out with existing military department budget authorities and would not increase outlays. Second, while there is a potential for some service members to be promoted later if they are not ranked high in a merit sequence, the additional wait would likely be no more than three to six months, depending on how much of a list the service intends to elevate based on merit.

One other consideration regards the extent to which the services would broadcast the fact that they were using a merit-based promotion sequencing system. The consensus was that, while they probably would not go out of their way to draw attention to resequencing based on merit, they would not hide it either. Officers at the top of the lineal list based on merit would therefore receive a subtle signal that they were considered high achievers.

Given the prevailing view that the benefits outweigh the costs, all four of the military services have endorsed a legislative proposal to amend Sections 616, 617, 624, 14108, 14109, and 14308 of 10 U.S.C. to allow for promotion selection boards to recommend officers for higher placement on promotion lists based on particular merit, if at least a majority of the promotion selection board members so recommend. However, because each of the services has unique officer selection and promotion practices based on service regulations and culture, the services also emphasized the importance of crafting an amendment with permissive language that would provide significant discretion to the service secretary.

To that end, a current legislative proposal emphasizes the need to provide flexibility and discretion to the service secretary and notes that the amendment would not limit the number of officers who could be moved to a higher lineal number based on merit. Services would be free to retain current lineal list policies, move 10 percent or 20 percent, or use some other construct approved by the Secretary of the Military Department for reordering the lineal standing of selected officers.

Service-Specific Approaches to Merit-Based Promotion Sequencing

We found that each of the services has its own views regarding implementation of merit-based promotion sequencing, driven largely by service culture and current processes for officer selection and promotion. Our overall findings are contained in Table 2.1 and can be summarized as follows:

- **Utilization:** While all of the services endorsed the legislative change, only the Army, Navy, and Marine Corps said they would take advantage of it if it became law. The Air Force would not immediately exercise the latitude, for reasons discussed later in this chapter.
- **Impact on active duty:** Of those services that would utilize their newfound flexibility, both the Navy and Army would choose to reorder up to the top 15 percent of their selectees based on merit, while the Marine Corps would elect to reorder the entire list of its selectees by merit.
- **Impact on reserve components:** The Army and Air Force require assignment to a position in a higher grade, discussed later, for some reserve officer promotions, which often results in immediate promotions at the beginning of a cycle rather

Table 2.1
Service Plans to Implement Merit-Based Promotion Sequencing

Service	Likely to Implement?	Impact on Regular Officers	Impact on Full-Time Reservists	Impact on Part-Time Reservists	Impact on National Guard Members
Army	Yes	Up to 15% of selectees sequenced by order of merit, remainder by date of rank	Up to 15% of selectees sequenced by order of merit, regardless of position of assignment	Up to 15% of selectees sequenced by order of merit, regardless of position of assignment	Up to 15% of selectees sequenced by order of merit, regardless of position of assignment
Navy	Yes	Top 15% of selectees sequenced by order of merit, remainder by prior lineal number	Top 15% of selectees sequenced by order of merit, remainder by prior lineal number	Top 15% of selectees sequenced by order of merit, remainder by prior lineal number	n/a
Air Force	Not immediately	n/a	n/a	n/a	n/a
Marine Corps	Yes	Reorder selectees by order of merit	Reorder selectees by order of merit	Reorder selectees by order of merit	n/a

SOURCE: Interviews with service personnel policy representatives.

NOTES: *Lineal number* is an indication of an officer's rank and precedence within a specific service. Date of rank is the primary determinant. For officers with the same date of rank, DoDI 1310.01 provides some differentiating criteria and leaves remaining differentiation to service secretary discretion.

than in monthly increments from the lineal list. That said, the Army plans to elevate up to 15 percent of Army AGR officers for promotion sequencing based on merit, regardless of position vacancies. Similarly, it would elevate up to 15 percent of its part-time reserve component based on merit, if given the authority to promote those so elevated without regard to position of assignment. The Navy and Marines do not require position vacancies for their reserve component promotions and would therefore conduct merit-based sequencing in the same manner as for their regular officers. The Air Force Reserve component would not be affected because it has no immediate plans to pursue merit-based promotion sequencing.

- **Impact on National Guard:** The Army National Guard (ARNG) and ANG condition promotions on position of assignment. The Army would sequence the top 15 percent of ARNG officers by merit, but assignment to a higher-graded position would take precedence and may lead to faster promotion than sequencing by merit. The ANG would not be affected because the Air Force has no immediate plans to pursue merit-based promotion sequencing.

Army Approach

Army officials were highly supportive of gaining the flexibility to reward their top performers with merit-based promotion sequencing. By giving their top performers a chance to be promoted earlier than under the current process, they hope to strengthen the signal to those officers that they are high achievers and also give them some extra time to pursue grade-dependent educational or assignment opportunities. That said, Army officials noted that they would limit the merit-based sequencing to no more than 15 percent of top officers. They would like to continue sequencing the remainder of the lineal list by date of rank to maintain a sense of camaraderie in the rest of the force.

If the proposed statutory change is adopted, implementation would be relatively straightforward. The following sections will explain how the Army selects and promotes officers today and how the change to merit-based sequencing would change those practices. The discussion first addresses the impact of merit-based promotion sequencing on Army active-duty officers and AGRs, then turns to the impact on part-time reserve officers and National Guard full- and part-time officers.

Regular Officers and AGRs

In a given promotion cycle, the promotion board considers all the APZ, IPZ, and BPZ candidates for vacancies within grade caps for a given fiscal year. To determine BPZ candidates, the board adopts a process known as BPZ integration. This involves selecting up to four times the quota of BPZ selections (for example, if the BPZ promotion selection quota is 50, the board would select 200 candidates) for consideration alongside IPZ candidates. The board then scores these BPZ candidates and all IPZ and APZ candidates and sequences them by board score. The highest-sequenced officers who meet occupation-based requirements for the fiscal year are selected for promotion, so long as they are deemed fully qualified. After all occupational requirements are met, the remaining officers on the list are selected in sequence until the overall selection quota is reached. In practice, this means that an infantry officer with a lower board score might be selected for promotion, whereas a higher-scoring armor officer might not, depending on how occupation-specific requirements match up to the sequencing of officers considered by the board. It also means that the BPZ candidates might end up ranking very high on the board-score sequence list and will almost certainly be selected when occupational requirements are applied; conversely, there will likely be BPZ candidates ranked too low on the sequence list to be selected.

The proposal to sequence the top 15 percent of selectees by merit would not require major changes to this process. The Army would use its current sequencing process (including APZ, IPZ, and BPZ candidates) by board score to determine the top 15 percent for merit-based sequencing. The remainder of officers selected for promotion would be sequenced by date of rank. The likely impact of this shift would be that the top 15 percent of selectees would be promoted earlier—around 5.5 months earlier for those high-merit IPZ selectees in the middle of the seniority range (see Figure 2.1).

BPZ selectees, who would likely be heavily represented in the top 15 percent due to their high performance, would stand to gain even more time in grade relative to their due-course counterparts. With a first BPZ selection, they would gain an average of about 18 months, and with a second selection they would gain a cumulative average of about 30 months compared with due-course officers (see Figure 2.2).

Part-Time Reservists and National Guard Full- and Part-Time Members

Most part-time reservists and full- and part-time National Guard members are selected for promotion on a best-qualified basis, with timing of promotions based on assignment to a higher-graded position. As discussed previously, part-time reserve officers who are selected by a mandatory promotion board (a promotion-zone-based board, comparable with a regular officer promotion board) may be promoted out of sequence to fill a vacant higher-graded position.

Turning to the question of merit-based promotion sequencing, if given statutory latitude regarding both sequencing of promotions and assignment to higher-graded position, the Army would plan to sequence up to 15 percent of its part-time reservists by merit, regardless of assignment to a higher-graded position. The remaining reservists would continue to be sequenced by date of rank, subject to assignment to a higher-graded position. The top 15 percent of ARNG full- and part-time officers could also be resequenced by merit, but assignment to a higher-graded position would continue to take precedence.

Navy Approach

Like the Army, the Navy fully supports merit-based promotion sequencing. Yet the Navy also acknowledged that, if adopted, changes would need to be made to its selection and promotion processes. Given the large number of candidates typically considered when a board convenes—upwards of 1,000—the Navy argued that it does not have the resources for the fine-grained decisionmaking needed to sequence more than 15 percent of the selectees by merit. In fact, as discussed further later, Navy officials felt that they would need to convene a separate board for merit-based promotion sequencing. The sections that follow explain how the Navy selects and promotes its officers today and how the shift to merit-based sequencing would change those practices. The discussion first addresses the impact of merit-based sequencing on active-duty officers, then turns to a discussion of its impact on reserve officers.

Regular Officers

For each annual promotion cycle, the Navy determines the number of promotions required in the following fiscal year, often based on budgetary limits that are below statutory grade ceilings. The number of candidates needed to provide the appropriate selection rate is then determined, with specific candidates identified by first and last lineal numbers. Within a promotion cycle, the board considers BPZ, IPZ, and APZ officers with no overt labeling of the zone of consideration.

The board assigns confidence factors to each record and then votes on candidates using a scoring system of 100, 75, 50, 25, or 0. The average score for each candidate determines his or her order of merit. Selectees are then promoted by date of rank, but the Navy uses a phasing system to space out monthly promotion increments for budgetary reasons. Under the phasing system, selectees are promoted in very small monthly increments (3 percent) for the first 11 months of the year, and then, in the twelfth month, the remaining 67 percent of the selectees are promoted.

Navy personnel managers anticipate that selection and merit ranking would be based on different criteria. Navy line officers are selected for promotion based on criteria related to suitability for command at sea. Navy officials believe that merit-based promotion sequencing should be based on broader criteria. Accordingly, the Secretary of the Navy would need to direct a second board process to place officers in merit sequence and identify the top 15 percent. Once this second process determined the order of merit, those individuals would be promoted in the first five months of the year (at a rate of 3 percent per month under the phasing system), and the remaining 85 percent of officers sequenced by date of rank would be promoted thereafter.

As was the case with the Army, the main impact of this shift would be that the top 15 percent would be promoted earlier, with many moving from the last month of the fiscal year to one of the first five months of the year and with BPZ candidates seeing even greater gains. But many officers (the most junior 67 percent who are not in the top 15 percent) would see no change in their promotion timing.

Reservists

The Navy Reserve uses the same promotion process as its active-duty counterpart, with a few exceptions. First, the Navy Reserve does not use BPZ promotions. Second, the reserve component uses a "running mate" system, which determines when officers are considered for promotion. Under this system, reserve officers are tied to an active-duty running mate to ensure that they are generally considered for advancement around the same time in their careers as their active-duty counterparts. Once the officers are selected for promotion, however, they are resequenced on the promotion list according to their date of rank and are matched up with a new running mate.

The Navy Reserve plans to mirror the active-duty component's approach to elevating the top 15 percent for merit-based promotion sequencing. Because the selection and promotion processes are nearly identical, they expect the impact to be about the same for the reserve component: the top 15 percent will be promoted more quickly, some will see slightly longer waits, and many (the most junior 67 percent who are not in the top 15 percent) would see no change. The Navy does not foresee the running-mate system having any real impact on merit-based promotion sequencing in the reserve component. Regardless of whether reserve officers are sequenced by merit or by date of rank, they are matched up with a new running mate once they are selected for promotion.

Marine Corps Approach

Like representatives of the other services, Marine Corps representatives said they supported merit-based promotion sequencing, noting that they think it will have an overall positive effect in rewarding high-performing Marines. While their selection and promotion process is somewhat similar to that of the Navy, they would choose to resequence their entire promotion list by merit because they are a smaller force and they feel this is a feasible proposition.

Regular Officers

The Marine Corps promotes officers in blocks throughout the year based on monthly vacancies within grade-strength ceilings. Officers, including BPZ, IPZ, and APZ candidates, are selected by a 21-member board. The board votes on each candidate. Officers who receive 21 yes and 0 no votes are at the very top of the list, followed by officers who receive a 20–1 vote, and so on.

The Marine Corps would capitalize on this existing process to sequence its promotion list by order of merit. Selected officers would be sequenced by merit based on their vote count (i.e., 21–0, 20–1, 19–2, etc.). Within each of these vote count groups, the officers would be sequenced by seniority.

Reservists

The Marine Corps would use an identical process for its reserve component. While the Marine Corps technically has a running-mate system like the Navy, the Marine Corps has been operating under a waiver from the Secretary of the Navy to deviate from this system.

Air Force Approach

While the Air Force offered full support for merit-based promotion sequencing reform, representatives said they would not choose to take advantage of the tool immediately. One reason for the Air Force's hesitation is its view of pay table reform. Service representatives argue that, in order to make merit-based promotion sequencing a significant reward for high achievers, it would need to be offered in tandem with a lasting pay increase relative to their due-course peers. Since pay is tied to time in service rather than time in grade, officers who are promoted BPZ experience only a temporary pay increase when they are promoted to a higher grade; once their due-course peers are promoted, they are all paid at the same rate again based on their grade and time in service. In the view of the Air Force, this phenomenon significantly diminishes the rewards for selectees who are promoted early, whether due to BPZ selection, merit-based promotion sequencing, or some combination of the two.

The Air Force is also refraining from immediate implementation of merit-based promotion sequencing due to the significant impact it would have on BPZ officers. Because the Air Force promotes BPZ eligibles up to the maximum of 10 percent of the number of officers considered for promotion in a given cycle (10 U.S.C. 616), merit-based sequencing could result in its comparatively large pool of BPZ selectees being promoted up to three years ahead of due-course officers (for those selected two BPZ). Additional time would be needed to assess the impact of this.

Regular Officers

Other reasons for the Air Force's hesitation to adopt merit-based promotion sequencing relate to its current selection processes. Unlike the other services, the Air Force conducts a separate selection process for its BPZ candidates. That means the Air Force would have to find a way to merge those BPZ candidates with IPZ and APZ candidates so they could be ranked by order of merit. A further complication for the Air Force relates to its use of multiple panels within a board. Each panel receives a proportion of the promotion quota and ranks a subset of officers by merit. There is no aggregate merit ranking of all the officers considered, except for a "gray zone" at the margin of each panel's share of the promotion quota. To level out quality differences in the distribution of records to the various panels, all panels vote on candidates in the gray zone.

Reservists and Air National Guard Members

For both its guard and reserve components, the Air Force promotes officers based on fully qualified selections and occupancy of higher-grade positions, and Air Force Reserve officials said they feel this gives them the flexibility they need to promote high performers quickly.

Summary: Promotion List Resequencing

Under DOPMA, officers advance through the grade structure based on a combination of merit and seniority considerations. Seniority determines when officers will be considered for promotion, and merit is the basis for determining who will be promoted. Once selections are made, seniority again prevails as the basis for determining the sequence in which officers assume the higher grade. This mix of merit and seniority undoubtedly has contributed to a sense of fairness and objectivity in promotion and career management processes. After reviewing proposals for allowing merit to play a greater role in promotion list sequencing, we believe useful talent management objectives would be served by them without undermining the real or perceived fairness and objectivity of the system.

In a military human capital management system, promotions provide the strongest and almost exclusive mechanism through which extrinsic rewards for performance are differentiated. Allowing merit to influence the sequencing of promotion lists provides a marginal increase in this differentiation. As indicated previously in this chapter, high merit is rewarded within a promotion cycle only to the limited degree that BPZ selectees are promoted an average of about half a year ahead of their due-course peers, after which their extrinsic rewards (pay) are again undifferentiated from their due-course peers'. Merit sequencing of the list would provide a longer period of higher pay for high-merit selectees—greater differentiation for BPZ selectees, lesser but still recognizable differentiation for non-BPZ high-merit selectees—modestly increasing the extrinsic rewards for their stronger performance.[5]

The services recognize that their promotion processes provide only limited means of discerning fine-grained differences in performance, and thus their expected processes for implementing merit-based sequencing would rely on a prudent blending of merit ranking and seniority.

While we see advantages in providing this flexibility, we don't see a downside. Since grade strengths will not change as a result of different promotion list sequencing, cost is not a consideration. The only negative consequence might be slightly less satisfaction with the promotion system among those not deemed to be of higher merit. However, as one service representative we interviewed pointed out, officers in the middle and at the lower end of the competitive spectrum are happy to be on a promotion list, regardless of where they might be sequenced on it.

On the broader issue of how the fairness and objectivity of the promotion system is viewed, it seems logical that if officers trust the promotion system to reliably select the best for promotion, they would also trust the system to select the best of the best for accelerated promotion. Proposed legislative changes specify a role for promotion boards in determining the rank orders used for merit sequencing. Thus, merit sequencing itself would retain all of the protections for fairness and objectivity that are built into statutory requirements for conduct of promotion boards. We believe it would be widely viewed by the most directly affected stakeholders—military leadership, military personnel managers, and military officers themselves—as a fair and beneficial step toward improved talent management.

Reporting Requirement: An Analysis of the Reasons and Frequency with Which Officers in the Grade of O-3 or Above Are Passed Over for Promotion to the Next-Highest Grade, Particularly Those Officers Who Have Pursued Advanced Degrees, Broadening Assignments, and Nontraditional Career Paths

If officers are passed over for promotion, it is generally attributable to one or more of the following causes:

- performance evaluations that indicate lesser performance or potential
- a negative indicator such as a weight management or behavioral problem

---

[5]   One service representative noted that the pay-related benefits of accelerated promotion would be greater if the pay table were based on time in grade rather than time in service. That would provide officers with accelerated promotions a lasting rather than a temporary increase in pay relative to their due-course peers.

- failure to complete an expected level of professional military education
- a pattern of assignments from which key crucible or developmental experiences are missing.

Promotion boards, however, do not identify specific reasons for nonselection. Thus, this reporting requirement must be addressed qualitatively rather than quantitatively.

Overall, the service representatives said they were not aware of any serious problems with officers above the grade of O-3 being passed over because of their choice to pursue advanced degrees or career-broadening assignments. In contrast, officers participating in nontraditional career paths, such as programs to allow pilots to pursue flying-only positions, were perceived to be at higher risk of being passed over for promotion. Officers generally have a better chance of promotion if they hit key milestones, such as command positions and professional military education, in a timely manner. The service representatives said that it was important for most officers to hit these milestones because they are there for a reason: to ensure the services are grooming officers who can lead forces in combat. Therefore, if officers pursued nontraditional career paths, they could be putting themselves at risk for promotion.

Advanced Degrees

Service representatives said they were not aware of any serious problems with officers above the grade of O-3 being passed over because of their decision to pursue a full-time master's degree. However, the service representatives did note that, due to their length, doctoral programs presented some promotion risk. They also noted that aviators at the grade of O-3 in the Marine Corps and the Navy also may face some promotion risk if they attempt to attend full-time schooling instead of operational flying because the latter is critical for promotion and also time consuming at that grade. In general, however, the service representatives tended to agree that full-time school is less of a risk if officers' careers are being monitored to ensure they hit necessary milestones and if those officers performed well in their last operational assignment before schooling.

Army Perspective

Army representatives said that, overall, they do not believe that Army officers who pursue full-time postgraduate education are disadvantaged. However, they noted that the Army officers who earn advanced civilian degrees are most likely to earn promotions if they are chosen for the most selective education programs, if they complete degrees in technical fields, or if they have strong performance evaluations before starting graduate school that will help them overcome a gap in their record due to schooling.

Army advanced degree programs can be divided into three categories: (1) highly selective education programs such as Joint Chiefs of Staff internships, congressional fellowships, and Olmsted Scholarships; (2) advanced civilian schools (ACS) to meet requirements to gain expertise in a given career field; and (3) the graduate school option, which is part of an Army recruitment effort known as the Career Satisfaction Program. The precommissioning program allows selected candidates to choose from three options in exchange for an additional active-duty service obligation: their first branch of choice, their assignment of choice, or a guarantee of full funding to attend graduate school in 6 to 11 years of service, after the candidate has completed key development milestones.

Army representatives said that officers in the first category were likely to be promoted due to the selective nature of their educational assignment. For officers in the other two categories, however, their competitiveness hinges on the strength of their performance evaluations before starting graduate school. Depending on the selectivity of the board, captains with middle-of-the-road files may be less competitive for promotion to major if they spend up to two years in graduate school immediately before they meet their major promotion board. Majors or lieutenant colonels enrolling in doctoral programs may similarly struggle if they have middle-of-the-road files. A secondary consideration might be the officer's career field and the type of degree: all things being equal, an engineer pursuing a functional degree might have an edge on an infantry officer pursuing a strategy degree that might be helpful but not essential for his or her career field.

All that said, however, officers in advanced civilian schools seem to do relatively well in the Army, at least at the master's degree level. In FY 2017, officers with ACS master's degrees overall were promoted at a higher rate (84.5 percent) than officers with other civilian education master's degrees (69.1 percent) or those with no civilian education master's degrees (69.8 percent).

Navy Perspective

Navy representatives said that, with the exception of aviators, the other career fields in its unrestricted line (surface warfare, submarine warfare, and special warfare officers) build in time for officers to attend advanced schooling, to include professional military education or a civilian master's degree. The officers who attend full-time graduate school are also chosen through a selective process that ensures they have competitive files for promotions later on.

Aviators in the grade of O-3, however, may not have time to attend full-time advanced education. Senior officers at the grade of O-3 incur promotion risk if they are not directly involved with flight operations and flying. In fact, Navy representatives said that the top pilots are typically assigned to "production tours," not graduate school, to ensure they have that flight experience under their belt when they meet their promotion board for O-4. Navy representatives said that allowing aviators to temporarily opt out of promotion boards, thereby gaining more time for school, might be helpful. Another way to prioritize advanced education, if the Navy wanted to do so, would be to put top pilots in graduate school, rather than a production tour, to send a signal of a cultural shift toward a greater emphasis on advanced schooling.

Air Force Perspective

In the Air Force, an assignment to full-time graduate school is generally driven by a functional requirement, and, as a result, it is looked on favorably by the promotion boards and time is built into the officers' careers to attend full-time graduate school.

Air Force officers who attend doctoral programs, however, may face some additional promotion risk because they are stepping off the traditional path for three years. In light of this consideration, Air Force representatives said they support an opt-out option to ensure those officers pursuing doctorates in science, technology, engineering, or mathematics (STEM) or other high-demand fields would have time to hit subsequent career milestones before being considered for promotion.

Marine Corps Perspective

Marine Corps representatives did not perceive a problem with officers getting passed over after attending full-time graduate school. Officer assignments are carefully tracked in the Marine Corps by monitors who ensure that high-risk candidates do not go to school until they have met essential milestones for promotion. In addition to carefully monitoring who goes to graduate school, Marine Corps representatives said they also ensure that advanced degrees are tied to requirements, thereby ensuring that the schooling will be valued.

The Marine Corps is also experimenting with a small pool of officers on a separate doctoral career track. These officers will not complete typical command assignments; instead, they will become strategists who provide insight to senior leadership. But the program is still small, consisting of fewer than five people, and still in its infancy, so the promotion prospects of these officers are still unclear.

Career-Broadening Assignments

Overall, the consensus was that career-broadening assignments do not present a promotion risk, and can even be career enhancing, as long as officers are able to hit their career milestones. With a few exceptions, this is possible because the services build in time for joint assignments or other career-broadening assignments and because these assignments are often highly competitive, which means the officers who complete them are also competitive for promotion.

Army Perspective

Army representatives said that career-broadening assignments are looked on favorably in the Army and therefore do not contribute to Army officers being passed over for promotion. In fact, junior officers are expected to take on career-broadening assignments to ensure well roundedness and to gain experience outside operations. Such experience might include an assignment at U.S. Army Training and Doctrine Command, Human Resources Command, or the National Training Center or serving as an aide-de-camp or as a legislative liaison. At the field-grade level, Army representatives said a broadening assignment might also involve joint credit under Goldwater-Nichols provisions. In short, Army representatives concluded that promotion boards generally look favorably on career-broadening assignments.

Navy Perspective

In the Navy, career-broadening assignments were viewed as positive as long as officers were also hitting their career milestones. A field-grade officer in the unrestricted line, for example, could complete a career-broadening assignment—such as a tour with industry—without risking promotion as long as he or she had already completed joint qualification and command assignments.

Air Force Perspective

Air Force representatives said they had no indications that officers who took career-broadening assignments, such as joint assignments or serving as ROTC faculty, were at risk for promotion. Like the other services, however, they offered the caveat that officers needed to be hitting their promotion milestones, and if career-broadening assignments were throwing them off track, they might be at risk for promotion.

Marine Corps Perspective

In the Marines, broadening assignments, known as "b-billets," are built into officers' careers to encourage the growth of well-rounded individuals and to give officers a break from operational assignments. Furthermore, monitors carefully track Marines' careers to ensure that any broadening assignment will be beneficial or, if it will not be, that the officer has been counseled on the risk. For example, the Royal Marine Exchange Program can present a promotion risk, but officers know this going in and may still choose to do the program anyway.

Nontraditional Career Paths

Representatives from each of the services agreed that there may be some promotion risk for officers who pursue nontraditional career paths, such as a series of combatant command–related assignments or programs that would allow pilots to assume flying-only positions. The problem with these nontraditional career paths, as mentioned earlier, is that officers may not have the time they need to excel at key career development milestones that make them strong candidates for promotion.

Army Perspective

Service representatives noted that they would support creation and management of alternate career paths for technical tracks. This process would allow those officers with technical skills in fields such as cyber, acquisition, or operations research/systems analysis to continue serving with different promotion time line requirements. However, Army representatives warned that if these new career paths result in better retention of officers in higher grades, the pool of officers authorized the alternate career path would need to be small to prevent stagnation in the promotion system. They also noted that they had not done any formal analysis to assess the impact on the promotion system. As such, they emphasized that the authority should remain in the hands of the secretary.

Navy Perspective

Navy officials said that they did not have much data on officers pursuing nontraditional career paths, such as tours with industry. However, they emphasized that any officer interested in pursuing such a path would be counseled by an assignment officer to ensure he or she is well aware of any risks. Navy representatives mentioned that aviators would be especially susceptible to promotion risk, should they choose a career-broadening assignment, because of the tight time lines for flight training and operational experience at the O-3 level. To that end, they said they support an option for aviators to opt out of the promotion process for a period of time so that they could complete their development as aviators and still do other kinds of assignments.

Air Force Perspective

Asked about what might constitute a nontraditional career path in the Air Force, service representatives offered the examples of an officer who had several combatant command assignments in a row, an officer completing a doctoral program, and an officer in a notional flying-only position. They contended that airmen on such nontraditional career paths may indeed face promotion challenges because they may miss various career milestones.

Air Force representatives said that officers with strong records could probably do one unusual assignment, but an extended pattern of nontraditional assignments would make promotions difficult. As a result, they would be interested in an opt-out option for officers pursuing nontraditional paths that would meet Air Force needs, such as doctoral candidates in STEM fields.

Marine Corps Perspective

In the Marine Corps, nontraditional career paths are not common because the Marine Corps operates on the Marine Air-Ground Task Force model, which ensures that every Marine is prepared for broader combat-related assignments. Both operational experience and career-broadening assignments are deemed essential.

Reporting Requirement: An Analysis of the Utility and Feasibility of Creating New Competitive Categories or an Independent Career and Promotion Path for Officers in Low-Density Military Occupational Specialties

The service representatives acknowledged that there may be a need to inject some additional flexibilities into the personnel system to manage some specialized career fields effectively. One approach would be to place these career fields in their own competitive categories. Another approach would be to add flexibilities within either separate or existing competitive categories. These flexibilities, which were made available to service secretaries through statutory changes in the FY 2019 NDAA, include allowing officers to opt out of promotion considerations temporarily, providing expanded constructive credit authorities, and providing for restructuring of promotions using alternative promotion authority. Several of these approaches could be combined with other proposed flexibilities to create separate technical tracks for some or all officers in these specialties.

Competitive Categories

The service representatives agreed that they already have the authority they need to create new competitive categories and that no additional legislative relief would be required. The Army, for example, recently created a new competitive category known as "information dominance" for the cyber mission. The Navy agreed that it has the authority it needs to adjust competitive categories and, in fact, can even shift officers between its restricted and unrestricted line competitive categories if needed. The service is currently considering whether to move at least one of its cyber warfare career fields to the unrestricted line, although there is some concern that those officers have fewer command opportunities and therefore may have some difficulty competing in the unrestricted line.

While Marine Corps representatives agreed that they had the authorities necessary to adjust competitive categories, they were not particularly interested in doing so in light of their recent experience creating a new financial manager competitive category. Marine Corps officials established the specialty because financial management Marines had difficulty competing for promotion, leaving gaps in critical assignments. But Marine Corps officers in the new competitive category reportedly have reacted negatively to the change because it requires them to be stove-piped in financial manager positions. They would prefer the previous structure, under which they served in financial management assignments with complementary broadening assignments available.

Opting Out of Promotion Consideration

This option allows individuals the opportunity to request to temporarily opt out of promotion consideration, thereby avoiding the stigma and possible involuntary separation consequences of nonselection, if important career milestones are missed due to advanced schooling, a career-broadening assignment, or a nontraditional career path. Each of the services supported legislation included in the FY 2019 NDAA (see Section 505) that gives service secretaries the flexibility to create this option, but they were fairly cautious about implementation. While the Navy and Air Force expressed interest in implementing opt out in a very limited set of cases, the Marine Corps and the Army were not interested in implementing the flexibility at this time. Across the services, there was a sense that the option to opt out of a promotion board could be abused by individual officers within the services if it were not tightly controlled. Furthermore, there was a concern that if too many officers opted out, it would clog up the promotion system. To the extent that there was an interest in implementation, service representatives called for the service secretary to retain the flexibility to selectively determine a specific pool of officers who could opt out and to set policy rules that would dictate the circumstances and duration under which an officer could opt out.

Army Perspective

Army representatives said that they would use the opt-out authority only in limited cases. The Army would limit the approval to an official of Headquarters, Department of the Army, to ensure (1) the volume of opt-out candidates does not negatively affect promotion opportunity for other officers and (2) officers do not use the opt-out authority to avoid the possibility of being nonselected for promotion.

Navy Perspective

Navy representatives said that they would implement opt-out flexibility on a highly controlled, limited basis. They said the option could be useful for aviators at the grade of O-3 who face a time crunch to complete a production tour and any kind of advanced civilian degree. Navy representatives offered the example of a lieutenant who chose to get a degree in Mandarin at the cost of her production tour. She was subsequently passed over for promotion, despite having developed what the Navy sees as valuable language skills. Navy representatives argued that if she had been able to opt out, the officer would have had more time to complete her production tour and get selected for promotion.

Air Force Perspective

Like the representatives of other services, Air Force officials said that they would support opt-out legislation but would want the service secretary to have the flexibility to determine whether to use it. Service representatives noted that while it might be beneficial to provide an opt-out option for officers pursuing STEM doctoral programs, they would like to limit the number of people in the program because they shared the Army's concern about promotion stagnation.

Marine Corps Perspective

Marine Corps representatives said they would support opt out but would be unlikely to use the authority. Because the Marine Corps is smaller, the service is able to assign career monitors to every officer, and Marine Corps officers have more time in grade to hit career milestones. As a result, they argued, Marines do not need an opt-out option to stay on track. Marine Corps representatives also shared the Army's and Air Force's concern that a large pool of officers opting out would create stagnation in the personnel system.

Constructive Credit

The service representatives were supportive of providing additional constructive credit to attract officer candidates in emerging career fields. However, while the Army, Navy, and Air Force representatives said they would likely implement the flexibility, the Marine Corps representatives remained undecided. Additionally, some service representatives recognized that constructive credit will have limited appeal in attracting highly experienced accessions because it is not used in basic pay determinations (10 U.S.C. 533).

   A direct-commissioning program for cyber officers, authorized under the FY 2017 NDAA, allows the services to provide three years of constructive credit to officer candidates. The service representatives support language in the FY 2019 NDAA that provides more constructive credit than that (up to the rank of O-6) because they have found that three years' credit is not enough to attract experienced individuals in the cyber realm, who can earn much higher salaries in the private sector. The service representatives also widely agreed that they would like to ensure that any legislation allowing for constructive credit remains open enough that service secretaries would be able to determine eligible career fields. NDAA language accommodates this desire because it does not specify career fields other than to say that secretaries should award the credit to individuals with training or experience that is directly related to "operational needs" (FY 2019 NDAA, Section 502). They saw this as a critical flexibility to ensure that as new missions emerge, there is a means to recruit professionals proficient in those missions with competitive salaries.

Technical Tracks

Broad service support exists for combining several potential legislative flexibilities to create technical tracks.[6] These career paths would be designed to recruit and retain officers with special skills that require deeper development and that might be in low

---

[6]   The opt-out and alternative promotion authority provisions codified in the FY 2019 NDAA provide means for developing promotion policies suitable for a technical track. The FY 2019 NDAA also included an amendment to DOPMA/ROPMA that would allow for the services to award more constructive credit. See Sections 502, 505, and 507 of the FY 2019 NDAA or Chapter Seven of this report.

supply, such as pilots or cyber warriors. In general, the concept of a technical track is to establish a discrete career path for a designated group of officers with high-demand skills who may be at a disadvantage when competing for promotion against more broadly developed and utilized officers. The new statutory flexibilities now available might allow these designated officers to meet promotion boards on more flexible time lines and with multiple considerations without being deemed "failed of selection."

Army Perspective

Service representatives noted that they would support, with some caveats, statutory flexibilities to allow for the creation of technical tracks through selective continuation. This process would allow those officers with technical skills in fields such as cyber to continue serving without meeting promotion boards. However, Army representatives warned that the pool of officers allowed to continue selectively would need to be small to prevent stagnation in the promotion system. They also noted that they had not done any formal analysis to assess the impact on the promotion system. As such, they emphasized that the selective continuation authority should remain in the hands of the secretary to prevent abuse.

Navy Perspective

Navy officials were relatively enthusiastic about new statutory authorities that enable the establishment of a technical track, but they called for additional legislative relief to make the system work. Referring to the concept as "up-and-stay," Navy representatives saw the technical track as a helpful way to retain aviators, providing some relief to their pilot shortage. Naval aviators would be able to continue on active service as lieutenants and serve as flight instructors. To alleviate concerns about stagnation in promotions, the total number of officers in the "up-and-stay" program would be limited to less than 5 percent of the officer corps. Navy officials said legislation also would be necessary to adjust pay tables, since officers in the program would not be receiving regular raises tied to promotions to the next rank.

Air Force Perspective

Air Force officials similarly supported the concept of a technical track for cyber and other emerging career fields. However, they shared the Army's concern that a pool of officers on a technical track could begin to clog up the promotion system. To mitigate this, they called for a legislative change to ensure that technical-track personnel—such as medical personnel—would not be counted against congressionally authorized grade tables. The Air Force was particularly concerned about how a technical track for additional career fields would affect its grade tables because it is the only service that promotes officers up to its full statutory grade ceilings. Air Force representatives also said it might make more sense to recruit civilians to perform emerging missions rather than to allow officers to stay at the same grade for long periods of time.

Marine Corps Perspective

While Marine Corps officials supported legislative flexibilities to establish a technical track, they were not convinced that the establishment of technical tracks would be the right approach for their service. Today the Marine Corps has only one large, competitive category that encompasses most of its officer force, based on the premise that every Marine should be able to assume the responsibilities of a Marine air-ground task force officer. As a result, Marine Corps representatives were hesitant to create a new competitive category for a technical track. It was also the view of Marine Corps representatives that Marines generally prefer promotions at regular intervals, along with the attendant opportunities for career-broadening assignments, staff jobs, and command positions, as opposed to one ongoing operational assignment.

Reporting Requirement: An Analysis of How the Armed Forces Can Avoid an Officer Corps Disproportionately Weighted Toward Officers Serving in the Grades of Major, Lieutenant Colonel, and Colonel and Navy Grades of Lieutenant Commander, Commander, and Captain, If Statutory Officer Grade Caps Are Relaxed

With the exception of the Marine Corps, all of the services' representatives were interested in flexibilities to relax the statutory grade caps. Their interest stemmed from two concerns. First, they argued that more flexibility to determine the number of officers at a given grade might be required to avoid promotion stagnation if they were to implement other options that would allow for more flexibility in the promotion system. The second reason the services—aside from the Marine Corps—were interested in flexibility in the grade tables was that they wanted the capacity to surge quickly in response to wartime needs. Service representatives argued that the authority to take greater control over the grade tables would not lead to disproportionate grade strengths because service budgets would ultimately limit the number of personnel at any given grade.

Army Perspective

Army officials said they would like grade tables to be replaced with a fixed percentage of officer strength for each of the field grades. The percentage would be based on analysis of grade distribution over the past 15 years, increased by a small amount to allow management flexibility during periods of service growth.

Navy Perspective

Navy officials were also interested in more flexibility within the grade tables. They argued that the services should entirely control the grade tables. In their view, there would be little risk of any particular grade ceiling becoming too bloated because budget constraints act as a limit.

Navy officials acknowledged that they do not operate anywhere near their grade ceilings, due to budget considerations, yet they would appreciate the increased flexibility. That way, in the event that they needed to surge quickly—and, presumably, their budget were increased to support that surge—they would not have to wait for congressional authorization to increase their grade strengths.

Air Force Perspective

Air Force representatives were also interested in some grade table reform, which they said would likely be necessary if they were to implement some of the proposed legislative flexibilities, such as the technical track. As the only service that operates up to its grade ceiling, the Air Force is particularly concerned about stagnation in the promotion system. To mitigate this, Air Force representatives shared the Army's support for legislation that would allow grade ceilings to be fixed in aggregate at the grades of major through lieutenant colonel. In addition, Air Force representatives also suggested that another solution might be to exempt certain competitive categories from counting against the grade ceiling, to include technical-track competitive categories.

Marine Corps Perspective

Because the Marine Corps operates well below its grade ceiling, representatives saw little need for adjustment to the grade tables. In fact, of all the services, the Marine Corps seemed to be the most cautious about implementing any additional flexibilities that might move its personnel numbers closer to its grade ceiling. Marine Corps representatives said they tended to prefer the relatively lean force structure they have adopted over time based on the DOPMA/ROPMA framework.

Conclusions

While there is some room for added flexibility in the promotion system, the service representatives indicated that, by and large, the seniority-based promotion system codified under DOPMA/ROPMA still works well. Across the services, there was a sense that the promotion system is producing officers who meet the requirements for commanding forces in wartime. Furthermore, while the service representatives were supportive of additional legislative flexibilities to manage their promotion processes, they were very cautious about implementation for fear of creating stagnation in a promotion system that they believe currently flows well.

However, the service representatives did see the need for some minor adjustments to accommodate the recruitment and retention of two types of officers in particular. First, they agreed that it would be reasonable to amend DOPMA/ROPMA to accommodate officers who gain additional education or career-broadening experience that would increase their value to the force. To that end, the service representatives supported now-enacted legislation to allow officers to opt out or additional flexibility to deem an officer "fully qualified" on condition of completing stipulated career milestones before promoting to the next rank (although they were not universal in their views of whether they would immediately implement the legislation). Second, the representatives widely agreed that there was a need to better accommodate officers in emerging mission areas such as cyber operators. In light of this concern, the service representatives were broadly supportive of flexibilities now available to develop technical tracks that provide alternatives to traditional promotion patterns and to offer constructive credit (although again, views on implementation were not universally shared). In all cases, however, the service representatives emphasized that while it could only be helpful for the service secretaries to have these additional statutory flexibilities, they need to be implemented in a controlled and judicious manner and targeted at only a small pool of officers. The service representatives argued that they have incentives to maintain a measured approach to the implementation of new flexibilities because the current system works well. It would be counterproductive, they argued, to apply these flexibilities to large numbers of officers because it could disturb, and even stagnate, the flow of officers through the promotion system.

CHAPTER THREE

Tenure

This chapter provides the service representatives' views on the need for DOPMA/ ROPMA modernization related to tenure management, including the "up-or-out" features of the promotion system and the standard 20-year path to retirement eligibility. It addresses the following five reporting requirements:

- a statistical analysis, based on exit surveys and other data available to the military departments on the impact that current personnel policies under DOPMA have on recruiting and retention of qualified regular and reserve officers of the armed forces; specifically, the statistical analysis shall include an estimate of the number of officers who leave the armed forces each year because of dissatisfaction with the current personnel policies, including career progression, promotion policies, and a perceived lack of opportunity for schooling and broadening assignments
- an analysis of the benefits and limitations of the current promotion time lines and the "up-or-out" system required by policy and law
- an analysis of the utility and feasibility of encouraging officers to pursue careers of lengths that vary from the traditional 20-year military career and the mechanisms that could be employed to encourage officers to pursue these varying career lengths
- an analysis of the current officer force–shaping authorities and any changes needed to these authorities to improve recruiting, retention, and readiness
- an analysis of any other matters the Secretary of Defense considers appropriate to improve the effective recruitment and retention of officers.

The next five sections of this chapter will discuss findings from the available data, as well as our interviews with service representatives. We examine the role of legislation in limiting the services' ability to retain officers, discuss where DoD or service policy—rather than legislation—may be the limiting factor, and provide proposed legislative changes from the services.

Reporting Requirement: A Statistical Analysis Based on Exit Surveys and Other Data Available to the Military Departments on the Impact That Current Personnel Policies Under the Defense Officer Personnel Management Act Have on Recruiting and Retention of Qualified Regular and Reserve Officers of the Armed Forces

This reporting requirement further stipulated that the statistical analysis shall include an estimate of the number of officers who leave the armed forces each year because of dissatisfaction with the current personnel policies, including career progression, promotion policies, and a perceived lack of opportunity for schooling and broadening assignments.

Our best resource for this issue was the Defense Manpower Data Center's Status of Forces Survey, available for both the active (SOFS-A) and the reserve (SOFS-R) components. The survey is conducted annually and features a large-scale representative sample (see Appendix B for selected results). The survey records individuals' perceptions regarding compensation, career options, and lifestyle considerations, along with demographic data regarding education levels, marital/family status, and pay grade. However, the survey does not collect respondents' branch of service. Therefore, the analysis is limited to exploring trends across all DoD service members. Analysis was conducted based on the SOFS-A and SOFS-R for 2016 (the most recently available data at the time of this writing).

Status of Forces Survey of Active-Duty Members

The SOFS-A asks a number of questions regarding service members' perceptions relevant to the impacts of DOPMA constraints. Item 20(c) asks respondents, "Taking all things into consideration, how satisfied are you, in general, with . . . your opportunities for promotion?" The answers are on a Likert scale ranging from 1 to 5, with 1 being "very dissatisfied" and 5 being "very satisfied."

Results for active officers across all grades suggest most officers were satisfied or very satisfied with the type of work they do (74.86 percent), the quality of coworkers (73.67 percent), and the quality of supervisors (73.46 percent). A smaller percentage of active officers were satisfied or very satisfied with opportunities for promotion (61.74 percent). Indeed, out of those who responded (2,928), just over half (52.46 percent) agreed or strongly agreed with the statement, "If I stay in the Service, I will be promoted as high as my ability and effort warrant," and over one-quarter (26.78 percent) disagreed or strongly disagreed with this statement. Consistent with this finding, out of those who responded (2,932), only 39.50 percent agreed or strongly agreed that the evaluation/selection system is effective in promoting its best members, and almost the same percentage (38.30 percent) disagreed or strongly disagreed with this. Also, out of those who responded (2,933), 61.85 percent of active officers agreed or strongly agreed with the statement, "I will get the assignments I need to be competitive for promotions."

Examining the results of active officers by grade reveals an interesting pattern. For satisfaction with opportunities for promotion, the expectation to be promoted as high as ability and effort warrant, the effectiveness of the evaluation/selection system for promoting its best members, and getting assignments needed for promotions, the percentage who were dissatisfied/very dissatisfied or disagreed/strongly disagreed all increased from O-1 to O-4, then decreased from O-4 to O-6 and above. This suggests that active officers at O-4 are the most dissatisfied with these aspects of promotion and assignment. Regarding satisfaction with the type of work done, the quality of coworkers, and the quality of supervisors, the percentage of active officers who were dissatisfied or very dissatisfied increased from O-1 to O-2, then decreased steadily to O-6 and above.

Items 163, 164, and 165 ask respondents for, respectively, the most important, second most important, and third most important factors affecting individuals' choices to stay on active duty. Respondents were provided a range of 42 options, including choice of jobs, level of challenge in their job, amount of personal time with family, pride in serving their country, and health care. The top five answers for all ranks combined were the military retirement system (13.96 percent), family concerns (7.08 percent), opportunities for career advancement (5.82 percent), pay and allowances (5.42 percent), and spouse/family attitudes (5.32 percent). Family concerns and spouse/family attitudes together constituted 12.4 percent. Special pay (such as retention bonuses) was the primary factor for only 1.92 percent of respondents (58 out of 3,024)—an interesting finding, given the cost of retention bonuses to the services and the perception that bonuses play a significant role in retention. Given the survey results, individuals making retention decisions are more likely to be concerned with family issues than with the presence or absence of a retention bonus.

At the individual grade level, junior officers indicated that they placed a higher weight on personal choice and promotion potential. Eight percent of O-1s and 6.65 percent of O-2s indicated that "choice of jobs" was their number-one consideration when deciding to remain in the military or leave. Those indicating that "personal choice/freedoms" were their primary consideration for staying in the military included 7.43 percent of O-1s, 9.14 percent of O-2s, and 7.2 percent of O-3s. Smaller percentages of officers at the O-5 and O-6 levels reported personal choice than did their younger counterparts but reported higher levels of family or spousal concerns; 6.3 percent of O-5s and 12.37 percent of O-6s reported "family concerns" as their primary factor for consideration, and 7.39 percent of O-5s and 10.75 percent of O-6s reported "spouse/family attitudes" as their primary concern.

Military retirement, while attractive across all grades, has the most marked effect on O-4s—24.06 percent of O-4s indicated that their primary consideration for staying on active duty is the retirement system. This aligns with the career time line, as individuals approach a higher likelihood of retirement eligibility and the prospect of attaining the grade of O-5.

"Opportunities to be assigned to station of choice" is the primary consideration for 5.26 percent of respondents. This is particularly true at the O-5 level, where 7.17 percent of respondents listed the choice as their primary consideration.

Status of Forces Survey of Reserve Component Members

The SOFS-R asks two questions particularly relevant to this study. First, item 40(c) asks, "How satisfied are you in opportunities for promotion within your unit?" and provides a Likert scale of 1–5 (very satisfied to very unsatisfied). Results for reserve officers suggest most were satisfied or very satisfied with their total compensation (78 percent) and the type of work they do (79.30 percent). A smaller percentage (66.19 percent) of officers were satisfied or very satisfied with opportunities for promotion.

Specifically, the percentage of reserve officers who were dissatisfied or very dissatisfied with their total compensation and the type of work they do steadily decreased from O-1 to O-6 and above. In contrast, the percentage of those dissatisfied or very dissatisfied with opportunities for promotion doubled from O-1 (6.78 percent) to O-2 (12.18 percent) and continued to increase till O-5 (14.62 percent), then halved at O-6 (7.01 percent).

Second, item 43 asks directly, "Suppose that you have to decide whether to continue to participate in the National Guard/Reserve. Assuming you stay, how likely is it that you would choose to do so?" Respondents are provided with a Likert scale of 1–5, with 1 being "very unlikely" and 5 being "very likely." Only 8.55 percent of respondents indicated that they were either unlikely or very unlikely to continue in the next six months. Guard and reserve junior officers reported the highest percentage of individuals unlikely or very unlikely to continue, O-1s (11.38 percent) and O-2s (12.32 percent).

Other Survey Research

In order to add to the robustness of the study, RAND researchers consulted the existing body of literature on exit/retention survey analysis.

In 2014, members of the Navy conducted an unofficial retention survey of existing service members from May 1 to May 30, 2014. The survey collected 5,536 responses out of the eligible 323,681 sailors. Sixty-nine percent of respondents indicated that they do not believe that junior personnel are utilized to their fullest potential, and they believe that this is a likely reason junior officers leave the service. Sixty-three percent believe that promotion is based on time in service rather than merit, raising questions about the fairness of the performance evaluation system (Snodgrass and Kohlmann, 2014, pp. 19, 23).

In 2015, the Air Force conducted the Military Career Decisions Survey, aimed at understanding the issues affecting pilot retention. The survey included Air Force rated officers in grades O-1 through O-5. Of the 41,599 officers eligible to take the survey, 13,641 completed the survey; 4,136 of the respondents were pilots, which served as the basis for analysis. Pilots reported frustrations with additional duties keeping them from flying. Many expressed a preference for a technical or "fly-only" track (Carson, 2017, p. 45).

Analysis

While the available data do not lend themselves to estimates of the number of individuals who leave the armed forces each year because of dissatisfaction with the current personnel policies, including career progression, promotion policies, and a perceived lack of opportunity for schooling and broadening assignments, they do provide useful indicators for policymakers. Most in the services are satisfied with their quality of life, coworkers, and supervisors, as well as their compensation. Officers express concern around matters of personal choice, including family concerns, the ability to remain in one location, and family/spousal attitudes when considering whether to remain in the military or separate. While DoD and the services may make reasonable accommodations to address these concerns, these issues may be beyond the control of the services. However, survey responses can inform better policy and practice regarding institutional practices. The percentage of individuals who do not think they will have the opportunity to promote to the level of their ability and effort (26.8 percent), the percentage of individuals who do not believe the evaluation and selection system promotes the best individuals (38.3 percent), and the percentage of officers who believe they will not receive the assignments they need for promotion (16.9 percent) are issues that the services can address. However, the services can improve these metrics independent of legislative change.

Reporting Requirement: An Analysis of the Benefits and Limitations of the Current Promotion Time Lines and the "Up-or-Out" System Required by Policy and Law

Overall, service representatives are in favor of maintaining the "up-or-out" system, which serves as the core component of DOPMA and ROPMA. Up-or-out is guided primarily by 10 U.S.C. 632, 10 U.S.C. 14505, and 10 U.S.C. 14506. Officers are promoted at key points in their career based on years of service. If twice passed over for promotion to any rank, officers are subject to being separated or retired (if eligible) from active duty unless selected for continuation through a board process or removed from the reserve active-status list. The up-or-out function of DOPMA and ROPMA is intended to emphasize a "young and vigorous" officer corps (Rostker et al., 1993, p. 3). By separating less competitive individuals at each promotion point, DOPMA and ROPMA ensure that the services do not become top-heavy and that competitive junior officers are able to promote through the system.

While the service representatives recognize that DOPMA and ROPMA pose some limitations on officer management in execution, there is consensus that up-or-out is an important feature for a healthy, vigorous force. DOPMA and ROPMA were initially created in part to help manage the problem of older, less competitive officers remaining at higher ranks, impeding the ability of junior officers to promote. Therefore, representatives from each of the services posited potential flexibilities to the current system while maintaining that the core of the up-or-out system should remain intact.

Further, in order to maintain a young and vigorous force, the existing statute stipulates that all individuals must retire by age 62 (10 U.S.C. 1251, 10 U.S.C. 14509).[1] Exceptions are currently made for those who pass the age limit, most frequently in more specialized career fields such as medical, chaplain, and judge advocate general. There is widespread support for lifting the age limitation.

Selective Continuation

While officers twice passed over for promotion face separation or retirement, the services do have the authority to continue individuals selectively if they are designated by a board convened for the express purposes of continuation (10 U.S.C. 637, 10 U.S.C. 4701). An officer selectively continued at the rank of O-3 may not be continued past 20 years of continued active-duty service or reserve active status unless he or she is promoted, and an officer at the rank of O-4 may not be continued on active duty or on the reserve active-status list past 24 years of active commissioned service.[2] The

DoDI 1320.08 further elaborates in policy what is laid forth in the law. The DoDI sets forth the minimum periods of continuation of active-duty officers as indicated in Table 3.1.

Army Perspective

Army representatives indicated a preference for maximum flexibility at the service secretary level. Flexibility would include authority to retain an officer beyond the current statutory limits of 20 years for O-3s and 24 years for O-4s. Representatives expressed that the added flexibility would likely be used sparingly in particular skill sets.

---

[1] FY 2019 NDAA, Section 501, removes the requirement that officer accessions must be able to serve for 20 years before reaching age 62. The requirement to retire by age 62 remains.

[2] Three sections in the FY 2019 NDAA may help address those twice passed over for promotion. Section 505, "opt-out" authority, may afford certain officers the ability to strengthen their files before being considered for promotion. Section 506 provides authority for officers in certain military specialties and career tracks in the grade of O-4 and above to remain in service up to 40 years. Section 507 provides an alternative promotion authority that allows for a larger number of promotion considerations before being deemed to have "failed twice of selection." See discussions in Chapter Seven.

Table 3.1
Minimum Periods of Continuation

Grade	Period of Continuation
O-3	Two years, unless the officer is within two years of qualifying for retirement, in which case the minimum period of continuation can be less. Officers selectively continued at the rank of O-3 cannot exceed 20 years of active continuous service.
O-4	Long enough to qualify for retirement if within six years. Officers cannot exceed 24 years of active continuous service.
O-5 to O-6	Shall not exceed five years, or when the officer reaches age 62.

Navy Perspective

The Navy indicated difficulties among the aviation community in making time lines for promotion. In large part, this is due to the significant career milestones that must be achieved in order for an aviator to be competitive for promotion to O-4. Aviators spend a significant portion of their early years in flight school, followed by a sea tour and a production tour. Therefore, they may be at higher risk for being passed over for promotion, and might benefit from increased flexibilities in selective continuation. However, selective continuation for this community is probably not the tool of choice; newly enacted flexibility to opt out of a promotion cycle may be preferable.

Air Force Perspective

Air Force representatives expressed a desire to use the current legal authorities to the best of their ability, keeping certain twice-deferred officers on active duty up to year 20 (for O-3s) and up to year 24 (for O-4s). However, the Air Force would like to have the flexibility to increase this limit and allow the services to retain technical talent selectively. Additionally, Air Force representatives favor the removal of age restrictions as set forth in DOPMA.

Marine Corps Perspective

Marine Corps representatives highlighted that the up-or-out system is necessary for the health of the service. In their view, up-or-out serves as a competitive forcing function, ensuring the quality of individuals being promoted at each rank. If an individual does not "make the cut," the current system leads to his or her separation at a lower rank.

While the Marine Corps representatives support selective continuation flexibilities for other services, they expressed that further selective continuation flexibilities are not necessary within their service. Since the Marine Corps career monitors closely manage officer assignment and development, Marine Corps representatives posit that each officer is clearly guided through the assignments process in order to keep him or her on the path toward promotion. Therefore, Marine officers generally are passed over for promotion for one of two reasons: (1) performance in their current assignment, or (2) self-selection out of promotion competitiveness. For example, promotion boards understand an individual's decision to decline a professional military education opportunity or other expected key developmental assignment as the choice to separate from the service at the next promotion point. Therefore, the Marine Corps would prefer not to selectively continue him or her.

Reporting Requirement: An Analysis of the Utility and Feasibility of Encouraging Officers to Pursue Careers of Lengths That Vary from the Traditional 20-Year Military Career and the Mechanisms That Could Be Employed to Encourage Officers to Pursue These Varying Career Lengths

The legacy retirement system, categorized as a defined benefit system, operates like a pension; service members do not contribute to a retirement plan but instead collect a certain percentage (beginning at 50 percent) of basic pay beginning at year 20. The military's new retirement system, the Blended Retirement System (BRS), enacted for all service members entering the force after January 1, 2018, contains both defined benefit and defined contribution components (DoD Office of Financial Readiness, 2017). Service members are still eligible for monthly retired pay for life after 20 years of service (at a lower rate than under the previous system), but contribute to their Thrift Savings Plan with matching contributions of up to 5 percent by the U.S. government. A one-time, midcareer bonus may be provided in the form of continuation pay, which—if invested in the Thrift Savings Plan—would add significantly to an individual's retirement. Unlike the 20-year eligibility requirement under the legacy system, BRS has a portable component, allowing individuals to separate with 401(k)-like transferability. Therefore, the BRS provides the services and DoD with an opportunity to rethink the standard career tenure, as more individuals might leave the service before 20 years.

Additionally, shortened military careers may reflect two different age and seniority distributions. Under the BRS, more service members may leave the service after fewer years of active service at lower pay grades, skewing the force younger than the current system. However, proposed changes to constructive credit and an end to age limitations that may increase the services' ability to assess officers at higher pay grades may yield a more experienced force beginning their careers at more-senior ranks before retiring under BRS with fewer than 20 years of active military service. A higher number of more-senior accessions could skew the force older (and/or more expensive) than the existing personnel management system. Across the services, there is widespread agreement that the impact of BRS is yet to be seen.

Shortened careers are not the only possible variance from the 20-year military career path. The services could also benefit from lengthened career paths, particularly for officers in certain functional areas, with advanced degrees, or on alternate career paths. Extended career paths would enable time for requisite education, language training, and utilization tours, producing competitive candidates for promotion. Extended career time lines might further enable extended assignment tenures, which may benefit particular career paths (such as foreign area officers [FAOs]). Extended career paths might also provide more time for broadening experiences that could benefit both the individual and the service. However, extended career time lines have the potential to increase costs and slow promotions to higher grades.

Under 10 U.S.C. 637a, the services maintain the flexibility to continue individual service members to 40 years of service. Such continuation is subject to the secretary of the military department concerned and allows the authorization of an officer in a grade above O-4 to remain on active duty if the officer has an MOS, rating, or specialty code deemed critical by the service secretary. These provisions, including criteria for designating the military specialties to which they apply, are subject to regulations prescribed by the Secretary of Defense. While this authority exists, data indicate that it is used sparingly. According to the DoD Office of the Actuary, in FY 2016 (the most recent year for which data are available), only 170 O-6s, 32 O-5s, and 5 O-4s retired with 30 years or more (DoD Office of the Actuary, 2017, p. 88).

Army Perspective

Army representatives indicated that a lengthened career path would enable flexibility for specific career fields. In particular, FAOs would benefit from being given the language training, graduate education, and experience that are difficult to fit into traditional career paths. However, Army representatives also highlighted that in order to plan to requirements, both accessions and attrition are part of the calculus. Flexibility in lengthened career paths should only be used to meet a requirement and should ensure that such flexibilities do not introduce stagnation into the promotion system. Army representatives noted that a process currently exists to extend careers beyond 30 years, but the Army is not currently using these authorities. Additionally, the Army supports lifting the age restriction as set forth by DOPMA and ROPMA.

Navy Perspective

Navy representatives indicated that the services need to rethink traditional retention profiles, particularly with the implementation of BRS. Navy representatives indicated that DOPMA currently provides the Navy with the flexibility to extend careers beyond 30 years, but that the Navy is not necessarily using the flexibilities. The Navy supports lifting the commissioning age restriction set forth by DOPMA.

Air Force Perspective

Air Force representatives indicated that as BRS provides more off-ramps for military service, they are looking for more on-ramps. In order to balance the potentially large off-ramp offered by BRS, the Air Force will likely rely on constructive credit, bringing in more individuals at higher ranks for a period of service. The Air Force supports lifting the retirement age restriction as set forth by DOPMA and ROPMA.

Marine Corps Perspective

With respect to the potential for shorter career paths, Marine Corps representatives emphasized that the impact of BRS on junior officer retention remains to be seen. The Marine Corps representatives are further unsure whether they would exercise increased flexibilities in constructive credit. Culturally, the Marine Corps values consistent training across all Marines and would prefer to grow its future leaders organically. Therefore, shorter careers skewed toward more-senior ranks are unlikely.

Additionally, given the way the Marine Corps manages officer careers—including the career designation board approximately 18 months after a Marine is promoted to O-3, separating those who do not meet quality standards before they reach O-4—many Marine O-5s remain in service until 28 years of service. Further, the Marine Corps operates well below its grade ceiling. As such, Marine officers already have a degree of flexibility to accommodate longer career paths.

Reporting Requirement: An Analysis of the Current Officer Force–Shaping Authorities and Any Changes Needed to These Authorities to Improve Recruiting, Retention, and Readiness

In the military, *force shaping* refers to the tools available to draw down force sizes and systematically manage retention profiles. Available mechanisms include selective early retirement boards (SERBs), voluntary separation pay, and temporary early retirement authority. It behooves the services to take a deliberate, strategic approach when they are reducing the size of their forces.

Under current statute, SERB authority is governed by 10 U.S.C. 638. Officers may be considered for early retirement if they are passed over for promotion to O-6 twice or if they remain in the grade of O-6 for at least four years and are not considered for promotion to general or flag officer. The service secretary is responsible for specifying the number of individuals recommended for early retirement. The number may not exceed 30 percent of the number of officers considered at each grade and in each competitive category. Currently, an officer may not be considered for selective early retirement more than once in any five-year period.

The services also have a temporary enhanced SERB (eSERB) authority, expiring in 2025, under 10 U.S.C. 638a. Used during times of drawdown, eSERB allows the secretary of a military department to consider service members for early retirement through a board if the individual has reached the grade of O-5 and has been passed over for promotion at least one time, as well as officers in the grade of O-6 who have been on active duty in that grade for two years. eSERB further enables the service secretary to consider those below the grade of O-5 who are retirement eligible within two years or less. The statute limits the number of individuals separated to 30 percent of the number of officers considered in each grade in each competitive category. eSERB further allows the secretary of a military department to manage the force more surgically by targeting all officers in a particular grade and competitive category, or all officers of a particular grade, competitive category, and year group. The determination should be made based on the needs of the service.

While current statute limits the authority of a service secretary to considering individual officers no more than once in a five-year period, the Secretary of Defense has the authority to authorize a service secretary to waive the five-year period. Some of the service representatives indicated a preference to conduct SERBs more frequently, ranging from annual SERBs (in the Navy) to SERBs conducted every three years (in the Air Force).

Across the services, there was widespread support for making eSERB a permanent authority for future use.

Army Perspective

The Army supports making the eSERB authority permanent. However, Army representatives did not think they would necessarily need the tool moving forward. The Army believes that, in practice, promotion boards are already used as a force-shaping tool well before a SERB is required, as evidenced by selectivity rates during a downsize.

Navy Perspective

Navy representatives support extending the eSERB authority permanently. Additionally, Navy representatives would like to use it for quality control, as well as force shaping. The Navy would prefer to see a change to the current legislation to allow consideration at one-year rather than five-year intervals in order to manage the force for quality.

Air Force Perspective

Air Force representatives supported the extension of the eSERB. Air Force representatives would like to see a change to the current legislation to allow consideration at three-year rather than five-year intervals.

Marine Corps Perspective

Marine Corps representatives would support the extension of eSERB but do not think it would necessarily be implemented within their ranks. This belief is due in large part to the Marine Corps's use of the career designation board at the O-3 level. The career designation board manages the active component officer population, identifying and retaining the best-qualified officers, and supports the promotion timing and opportunity to O-4 (Garza, 2014, p. 9). Individuals are evaluated when they are IPZ to O-3 and must have 540 days of observed fitness report time following their initial occupational specialty training. Based on selection rates, career designation is more competitive than the rates of promotion to O-4. Therefore, the pool of candidates considered for promotion to O-4 has already been screened for quality in a process that differentiates the Marine Corps from the other services. The Marine Corps is then able to promote nearly all career-designated captains to the rank of O-4. In the opinion of Marine Corps representatives, this practice keeps faith with individual service members. The due-course Marine is promoted to the rank of O-4 after ten years of active-duty service. In the Marine Corps representatives' estimation, by the time an individual reaches the rank of O-4, he or she has invested heavily into the Marine Corps; to separate a noncompetitive candidate after ten years of service with no retirement (under the legacy retirement system) is deemed a break in faith. The Marine Corps finds it more tenable to separate those who do not meet the quality standard at an earlier rank.

By winnowing the number of field-grade officers earlier in their careers, the Marine Corps does not currently reach its authorized field grade strengths. Therefore, the Marine Corps has less need to execute SERBs and only uses them as a last resort.

Reporting Requirement: An Analysis of Any Other Matters the Secretary of Defense Considers Appropriate to Improve the Effective Recruitment and Retention of Officers

While Secretary of Defense James Mattis has not explicitly laid forth specific personnel management reforms, two of his stated priorities have implications for officer retention: deployability and lethality.

Emphasis: Deployability

On February 14, 2018, Under Secretary of Defense for Personnel and Readiness Robert Wilkie released a memorandum updating the DoD retention policy for nondeployable service members (Wilkie, 2018). These policies have been promulgated in a recently released DoDI, *Retention Determinations for Non-Deployable Service Members* (DoDI 1332.45). Previously, in July 2017, the secretary had directed the Office of the Under Secretary of Defense for Personnel and Readiness to lead an effort to identify changes to military personnel policies in order to provide more "ready and lethal forces." The secretary laid forth two priorities: a reduction in the number of nondeployable service members and an improvement in readiness across the services.

The study determined that those service members who were nondeployable for more than 12 consecutive months (with the exception of pregnant and postpartum service members) would be processed for administrative separation. Service secretaries were authorized to grant waivers in certain cases. The secretary stipulated that the services have until October 1, 2018, to begin the mandatory processing of nondeployable service members.

In addressing the update to policy, Secretary Mattis emphasized deployment equity across the force. If individuals are unable to deploy, the end result is a higher deployment rate for those who are able to deploy. The secretary emphasized that current policies were strong enough; they simply needed to be adhered to more strictly (Moon Cronk, 2018).

The emphasis on deployability may work in tension with retention. While performance metrics may factor into an individual's inability to deploy, it is more likely that medical issues will result in nondeployability. The renewed emphasis on deployability may result in separating individuals who otherwise make useful contributions and who may become deployable in the future. However, the services maintain that the waiver authority at the service secretary level allows for flexibility. Additionally, the services do value deployability in their service members.

Emphasis: Lethality

Under former Secretary Mattis, DoD's number-one priority was increased lethality across the services. The secretary emphasized "combat preparedness, lethality, survivability, and resiliency" of ground close-combat formations (Mattis, 2018). He directed large investments in front-line technology, including improved body armor, rifles, and night-vision goggles.

In addition to technological improvements, the secretary's emphasis on lethality also has two management components. First, the department is focusing on increasing unit cohesion by keeping units together longer. Culturally, the services have penalized individuals for remaining in one job for an extended period of time (Freedberg, 2018). If the services—particularly the ground elements of the Army and Marine Corps—pursue longer time lines for assignments across specific units, they will need to consider ways to ensure promotability for officers in those units in light of how these lengthened assignments might reduce their breadth of experience or interfere with completion of other milestones considered important for promotion. Second, the secretary's focus on lethality prioritizes combat training above other experiences. The emphasis on training may detract from broadening opportunities. While the emphasis on combat training has the benefit of creating tactical expertise, it is worth considering that the services also benefit from investing in individuals to build strategic expertise.

Conclusions

Consistent with our findings on other topics, the service representatives agreed that with respect to tenure management, DOPMA/ROPMA provides a solid foundation for personnel management. While the services are open to increased flexibility, they maintain that the fundamental nature of the statutory up-or-out system is effective.

Where the services are pursuing tenure flexibilities, two themes emerge. First, while increased flexibilities are desirable, the service representatives still prefer a high threshold for executing any new authority or flexibility: approval at the service secretary level. Second, each of the service representatives articulated that flexibilities should be exercised based on the needs of the service and must be tied to requirements. While the increase in tenure flexibilities may provide retention incentives and increase officer career satisfaction, implementing the flexibilities must serve or at least be consistent with the needs of the service—not simply to accommodate individual desires.

Lastly, the service representatives maintained that DOPMA was initially created as the solution to a variety of officer management problems. As such, the service representatives are cognizant that any reforms or efforts to modernize DOPMA must not invalidate the gains DOPMA has brought to officer personnel management since 1980.

CHAPTER FOUR

Talent Management

We grouped the following three NDAA reporting requirements in a bin we labeled "talent management":

- an analysis of the extent to which current personnel policies inhibit the professional development of officers
- an analysis of the efficacy of officer talent management systems currently used by the military departments
- an analysis of how best to encourage and facilitate the recruitment and retention of officers with technical expertise.

We note that *talent management* has taken on a range of possible meanings in recent usage. In some contexts, *talent* is equated with general ability; hence, *talent management* is equated with development and utilization of high-performing or high-potential individuals. In other contexts, *talents* are equated with specific combinations of knowledge, skills, abilities, and other attributes (KSAOs). Talent thus becomes highly personal, with combinations of KSAOs unique to an individual. While general ability may translate from one assignment to any other assignment, talent as KSAOs may be more suited for some assignments than others (Barno and Bensahel, 2015; Markel et al., 2011, p. 92). Talent management becomes the development of needed KSAOs and matching individualized KSAOs to specific requirements.[1] In still other contexts, *talent management* is used as a synonym for human resource management in general, or perhaps the more strategic aspects of human resource management, with a goal of producing desired long-term personnel outcomes. In our discussions in this

---

[1] The military services often employ this definition of *talent management* in official usage. For instance, the Army defines *talent management* as "a deliberate and coordinated process that aligns systematic planning for the right number and type of people to meet current and future Army talent demands with integrated implementation to ensure the majority of those people are optimally employed" (U.S. Army Office of Economics and Manpower Analysis, 2016). Similarly, the Navy uses *talent management* to mean "recruiting, developing and retaining the right number of Sailors with the right skills to man our force demands" (Navy Personnel Command, 2017).

chapter, we did not confine ourselves to one of these definitions but rather allowed the term to assume meanings appropriate to the issue at hand.

Current law provides wide latitude to the services on how they develop and assign their officers. DOPMA and ROPMA do not dictate a methodology for identifying talent or prescribe a system for matching officers with requirements, for instance. Aside from Goldwater-Nichols requirements pertaining to joint assignments, DOPMA and ROPMA do not recommend some assignments or experiences over others. They do, however, use constraints that shape how the services approach professional development and talent management. Three significant constraints shape the talent management environment:

- cohort management
- the composition of promotion boards
- the up-or-out tenure management system.

Promotion zones are established as the basis for promotion eligibility in 10 U.S.C. 623 and 10 U.S.C. 14305. Promotion zones provide a mechanism through which officers with similar time in grade and in the same competitive category enjoy "relatively similar opportunit[ies] for promotion." The use of promotion zones enshrines the concept that officers in the same competitive category should progress through their careers at relatively the same pace. The law provides opportunities for active-duty officers who are "exceptionally well qualified for promotion" (10 U.S.C. 619) to compete for promotion earlier than their peers, but the use of such BPZ promotion authority differs across services. The key aspect, however, is the codification of the idea that similar officers should progress at roughly the same rate.

Sections 612 and 14102 of 10 U.S.C. determine the membership of a promotion board, limiting the board's composition to "five or more officers of the same armed force as the officers under consideration by the board." A promotion board's members carry the responsibility of determining which officers deserve promotion to the next rank. As a result, the promotion board's members, within the broad outlines of secretarial instructions to boards, determine which traits and experiences carry more value than others. The promotion board's decisions shape the next generation of officers. Given a certain level of predictability in promotion board behavior over time, the services will craft career pipelines that meet the expectations of their promotion boards. Other board compositions, not currently authorized by DOPMA or ROPMA, would shape alternative outcomes. For instance, a promotion board with civilian representation might approach the diversity of assignments differently. In a separate example, a promotion board with sister service representation might approach assignments with other services in a different manner from current promotion boards.[2] Overall, a promotion board under its current construction rewards certain manifestations of potential and performance, knowledge of which the services then use to manage their personnel.

Sections 632, 14505, and 14506 of 10 U.S.C. establish the up-or-out promotion system, through which officers twice nonselected for promotion to O-4 or O-5 are involuntarily removed from active duty or the reserve active-status list. Though obviously a key tenet of tenure management, the up-or-out system constrains experimentation in talent management and adds a sense of urgency to professional development. Promotion zone provisions ensure that officers will move through their careers at the same pace, while up-or-out provisions establish penalties for those who move at a slower pace. The services respond to the up-or-out system through the way they manage their personnel. An officer has a defined window during which to demonstrate readiness for promotion. When constrained by the expectations of the promotion board, the service must shape professional development within the limits of the available time.

Thus, DOPMA and ROPMA affect talent management in three primary ways:

- Similar officers move through the promotion system at the same pace, except when promoted BPZ.
- Officers are considered for promotion by promotion boards comprising officers from their service.
- Those officers who do not meet the thresholds of potential and performance as seen by the promotion board are subject to being separated by the up-or-out system.

Reporting Requirement: An Analysis of the Extent to Which Current Personnel Policies Inhibit the Professional Development of Officers

Background

An investigation of professional development should begin with an understanding of definitions and concepts. The concept of professional development carries two intertwined themes: it is preparation for the future (a method), and it is preparation with a purpose (an end state). Professional development implies a set of actions taken with a goal in mind. A brief understanding of both themes will assist additional discussion.

Professional development entails a sense that one is acquiring useful experiences for the future. Such experiences are nearly limitless in their potential combinations: key assignments within a career specialty, graduate education, broadening tours with their

---

[2] DoD policy already requires joint representation on promotion boards for midcareer and senior officers. DoDI 1320.14 requires that promotion boards that consider joint officers include an officer nominated by the chairman of the Joint Chiefs of Staff to serve on the promotion board.

own myriad possibilities, exposure to senior military leaders, and much else. There is broad disagreement in blogs, discussion forums, and recent books over the sort of experiences that are required for the future or where shortfalls exist.[3]

Similarly, the goals of professional development matter. The first goal could be tactical competency within a career specialty. Within that framework, an officer will move through assignments of increasing responsibility and continually build experience and competence within a given career field. By the time the officer leads a large tactical formation, that officer will have many years of experience in varied roles within similar organizations. A related but separate goal could be the eventual management of some part of the defense enterprise. Additionally, notions of how these concepts interrelate bear witness to intense discussions.[4] Demonstrated tactical competency may be a requirement for eventual leadership in the defense enterprise, but then again it may not.

The constraints of DOPMA and ROPMA (cohort management, promotion board composition, up-or-out) influence professional development policies. Cohort management moves officers through their careers at a similar pace. As a result, the services developed personnel policies that could be uniformly applied to swaths of officers concurrently. Officers with similar time in grade will face the promotion board at the same time, and thus personnel policies reflect the consolidation of personnel management time lines. Every officer in a given competitive category with a similar time in grade must show adequate professional development on the same time line as the peer group. The weighting of some assignments over others reflect differences in service culture, but the standardization of personnel policies reflects a constraint of DOPMA and ROPMA.

Similarly, the promotion board composition underscores professional development policies. The membership of a promotion board matters, given that the members' experiences and expectations will manifest in the officers who are selected for promotion. Personnel policies, in turn, may reflect the outcomes of promotion boards. If a promotion board expects that successful officers will possess certain experiences, and the services can ascertain that preference, personnel policies will enable professional development along those lines. The result may be standardization of outcomes, with a uniformity in experiences across those who are promoted. Differences in service culture will emerge in the desired traits and experiences that emerge from a promotion selection list, but the standardization of expectations and resulting elimination of professional diversity reflects constraints of DOPMA and ROPMA.

---

[3]   Discussions occur in mass media publications and on specialized websites. The *Atlantic* published articles by Barno and Benashel (2015), as well as Tim Kane. Specialized websites with robust discussions of talent management include *War on the Rocks* and Thomas Ricks's *Best Defense* blog on *Foreign Policy*.

[4]   As an example, Barno and Benashel (2015) stated that "the skills of an effective Pentagon staff officer have next to nothing in common with those of an Apache attack-helicopter pilot or an infantry-battalion commander."

Lastly, the up-or-out system influences professional development policies. If promotion is the carrot that rewards professional development, separation is the stick that punishes noncompliance with expectations. This noncompliance may come from separate sources. On the one hand, some officers may not exhibit the potential and performance desired for service at the next-highest grade, at least as compared with their peers. On the other hand, some officers may not have the valued experiences desired at the next-highest grade. The up-or-out system could discourage officers from pursuing less traditional paths, and provides a severe outcome for those who fail to meet promotion standards. Service culture dictates how the services and promotion boards view less traditional paths, but the up-or-out system in DOPMA and ROPMA provides a potentially severe penalty for experimentation.

Themes
In May–June 2018, RAND researchers conducted a series of interviews with representatives of the Army, Navy, Air Force, and Marine Corps to gain insight into the talent management questions. The interview sessions included representatives from the services' personnel policy offices and often from personnel assignment centers. Several themes emerged from the discussion.

Documented Requirements Drive Professional Development Needs
The service representatives consistently highlighted that their professional development policies are driven by documented requirements. The operative word is *documented*, which implies that the requirement is known, identifiable, and quantifiable. Professional development thus proceeds from an evaluation of requirements, rather than requirements conforming to professional development. One could expect a lag between the identification and documentation of a requirement and the resulting changes to professional development.

Professional Development Models Are Generally Optimized to Produce Capable and Credible Leaders in Their Respective Career Fields
The service representatives consistently highlighted that their professional development policies focus on developing the tactical warfighting function, and they see this as both a key task and a point of pride.

Promotion Time Lines Are a Constraint
Unsurprisingly, the limited amount of time at each grade level forces the services to prioritize aspects of professional development over other areas. The constraint may be felt the most in training-intensive technical fields, such as aviation, where officers will spend years in training before gaining operational experience.

There Is Some Conflict Between Developing Tactical Leadership and Developing
Strategic/Enterprise Leadership, as Those Skills May Not Be the Same

The service representatives mentioned that, while their systems are optimized for the production of tactical excellence, they are less clearly oriented toward development of leadership competencies required beyond the tactical level. Service representatives were split as to their concern over this, with some believing that their professional development policies resulted in the development of the right leaders for all echelons, whereas others expressed concern.

Army Perspective

In our interview with Army experts, they emphasized that their standardized model of professional development produces the tactical leaders that the Army needs. Using assignments of increasing responsibility and an emphasis on serving with troops in a warfighting capacity, the Army routinely and systematically grows leaders for its tactical formations.

The Army allows requirements to drive broadening opportunities. Army experts used the example of the engineer branch to illustrate the point. To determine how many members of the engineer branch should have the education and experience that will allow them to qualify as professional engineers, the Army will first look to its requirements for professional engineers. These requirements, which necessitate coding identified billets for the qualification, will set in motion the process through which the Army will provide the education and experience to selected officers. Broadening thus becomes purpose driven, toward the goal of fulfilling requirements.

Looking toward the identification of senior leaders for strategic or enterprise assignments, the Army experts expressed some concerns regarding their professional development model. They mentioned that the model successfully provides numerous candidates for corps commander positions but few nominees for a position such as the Army G-8 or the Army cyber commander. The professional development model for corps commanders matches the standard path of professional development, with positions in combat-focused battalions, brigades, and divisions contributing to an officer's preparation. Unique positions such as the Army G-8 require preparation outside the traditional warfighting community, and the standard professional development model serves that requirement less well.

The Army experts mentioned that the Army could change the outcome of its professional development model, and thus change what a standard O-5 or O-6 looks like, with a change to the culture of its promotion boards.

Navy Perspective

Navy interviewees provided comments similar to those we heard from the Army regarding the effectiveness of its standard professional development model. As with the Army, the Navy emphasizes assignments within an officer's specialty with the goal of capable and competent leaders in that specialty. The Navy emphasized the technical aspects of competency, such as how effectively commanding a ship requires detailed knowledge and experience of the technically sophisticated systems aboard the ship. Such expertise arises from a career spent in similar environments, and the Navy's professional development model produces such outcomes.

The Navy experts raised a concern regarding the up-or-out system, particularly regarding career fields such as aviation with longer-than-normal training time lines. Officers in aviation will spend several years in training before their first operational assignment. Because of the standardization of career time lines under DOPMA and ROPMA and the penalties associated with missing a promotion gate, naval aviators face limited available time for professional development in the years immediately after initial training.

Like the Army representatives, the Navy experts mentioned that their standard professional development model may struggle to produce officers with the experience necessary for strategic or enterprise management assignments. They mentioned that Goldwater-Nichols joint requirements imposed a constraint that limits flexibility for officer development. The opportunities for broadening focus on meeting joint requirements, at the expense of other types of experience.

Air Force Perspective

Air Force interviewees emphasized that their professional development model produces officers capable of leading operations within their career fields. Unlike the Navy experts, Air Force experts were less concerned that training time, when interacting with the up-or-out system, results in undesirable outcomes. Given that flying is central to the Air Force culture, the Air Force may be less susceptible to this aspect of DOPMA or ROPMA. Air Force promotion boards and the Air Force professional development model may be able to fully appreciate the training time requirements, given that the core of the Air Force faces similar circumstances. For the Navy, where aviation provides an important capability but one that is complementary to its core as a sea service, aviation may be just unique enough that it struggles to fit into a normal career path.

Echoing comments heard from other service representatives, the Air Force experts stated that requirements drive broadening opportunities. The Air Force links its broadening assignments to needed capabilities and thus ties educational opportunities and assignments outside the core of a career field to identified requirements.

The Air Force experts felt that their standard professional development model adequately produces officers who can capably serve in strategic or enterprise management roles. More so than the representatives from the Army or Navy, the Air Force experts stated that their service generally produces the officers necessary for those positions, using their professional development model. Like the Navy experts, the Air Force experts mentioned that Goldwater-Nichols joint requirements constrain opportunities for broadening, or at least limit their discretion in how they broaden their officers.

Marine Corps Perspective

We heard from Marine Corps experts that their professional development model produces leaders who, as the experts stated, have "MOS credibility." That credibility arises from repeated and sequential exposure to positions of increasing responsibility. The experts noted that theirs is a performance-based culture, with those who demonstrated a high standard of performance being selected for positions of increasing responsibility. The Marine Corps experts described their professional development model as a well-developed path that is suited for producing the leaders that the corps needs.

The Marine Corps experts emphasized the size of the Marine Corps and the influence that its size has on its approach to broadening. The experts mentioned that the Marine Corps has more enlisted personnel per officer than other services. As a result, the Marine Corps must critically approach broadening assignments that remove officers from the Marines. There are not many Marine officers, and the absence of one is felt. Broadening, as with the other services, is tied to requirements.

The Marine Corps experts noted that their professional development also produces the leaders that the corps needs for strategic or enterprise management roles. The experts noted that because the Marine Corps is smaller and has a lower density of officers, the service cannot afford to have many officers follow nonstandard career paths.

Conclusions

The services have devised standardized career paths that effectively develop tactically proficient leaders. Those career paths account for facets of DOPMA and ROPMA that constrain professional development models, such as cohort management and the up-or-out system. Standardized career progression may place a burden on career fields that require additional training. Relaxing those constraints can change professional development models as currently employed, such as by allowing additional time for training-intensive career fields. Unknown, and a topic for future study, is what effect a change in professional development timing would have on officer retention.

While there is general satisfaction with most of DOPMA's and ROPMA's professional development implications, changes to DOPMA and ROPMA could change the relationship between the development of tactical expertise and that of strategic expertise. There is some indication that tactical expertise crowds out the development of strategic expertise, especially early in a military career. As the Army mentioned, changes to a promotion board's culture could change professional development models. A potential topic for future study is alternative promotion board membership schemes, which could potentially introduce new and varied interests into officer professional development.[5]

---

[5] Everett S. P. Spain (2014, p. 65), in his study on identifying and retaining high-potential officers, recommended adding one senior civilian from outside the service to a promotion board to bring an outside perspective to the proceedings.

Reporting Requirement: An Analysis of the Efficacy of Officer Talent Management Systems Currently Used by the Military Departments

Background

As discussed at the beginning of this chapter, *talent*, as in talent management, means different things to different audiences. These alternative discussions often contribute to frustration with current personnel policies. To explore this issue comprehensively, we considered the multiple meanings attached to this term.

Many criticisms of talent management systems currently employed by the services question whether a system that initially evolved after World War II and was refined with DOPMA (Rostker et al., 1993) can meet the requirements of today's armed forces. For instance, Barno and Bensahel (2015) question the continued utility of "[t]he current military personnel system [that] was designed decades ago in large measure to provide interchangeable human parts to fit the diverse requirements of each service." They question whether standardized career paths, predictable promotions, and a focus on generalized ability can adapt to changing requirements.

Tim Kane, a Hoover Institution researcher and former Air Force captain, also questioned the utility of the talent management system. In a survey of leadership and talent characteristics, he found that the U.S. military scored very low in three areas related to talent management: "[P]ay is closely aligned with performance; local supervisors have primary hiring authority, not central bureaucracy; bonuses are used effectively to reward good work" (Kane, 2017, pp. 20–22).

Themes

RAND researchers interviewed service representatives about their talent management systems, using the same interview period to address other talent management questions. Four themes emerged from the discussion.

The Definition of Talent Matters for the Discussion

Different perspectives emerged as to whether talent is general ability or a unique combination of KSAOs. These differences informed alternative perspectives to job matching and assignment slating.

Some Conflict Exists Between Talent as a Level of Performance and Talent as Unique Skills

Blending the two perspectives can be challenging, particularly when the promotion system focuses on an overall level of performance and potential.

Requirements Drive Talent Alignment, but Unit Signaling May Lag

All of the service representatives highlighted that theirs is a requirements-driven assignment process, but some service representatives noted that updated information regarding requirements can significantly lag behind assignment decisions. For services looking to match individuals based on KSAOs to jobs requiring those KSAOs, incomplete unit information can lead to suboptimal outcomes (Rostker, 2015, p. 3).

There Is Ongoing Movement Toward More Individual Matching, but Some Talents May Not Provide Institutional Benefits

As noted, some services are moving toward matching officers with assignments based on KSAOs. There was broad agreement, however, that some talents may not benefit the service. Service representatives highlighted that such talents could be certain educational pursuits, as an example.

Army Perspective

The Army is moving forward with matching individuals based on unique KSAOs with job requirements. The Army developed a web-based platform called the Assignment Interactive Module 2.0 that allows officers to highlight individual skills, characteristics, education, certifications, and career aspirations that may normally be ignored in talent management systems. Units with validated manning vacancies can view officers' profiles and express interest in officers. Assignment officers at Human Resources Command then use that information when making assignment decisions.

Army experts recognized that shifting talent management to a KSAO focus is a long-term effort. One expert noted that officers who commissioned in 2012 are the first generation that will have grown up in an environment in which KSAOs are prioritized. Until that generation rises to senior leadership positions, the shift will not be complete. The Army experts' comments reflect the observation on innovation in the military made by Rosen (1991, p. 105), who noted that "the process is only as fast as the rate at which young officers rise to the top." That said, the Army experts stated that operational requirements receive priority.

As the Army has moved to a KSAO focus, units have been slow to provide detailed requirements that reflect the KSAOs required for a certain job. As a result, assignment officers at Human Resources Command are attempting to match highly unique individuals with assignments that may be indistinguishable. The underlying cause of the unwillingness is unknown. Possible causes include a time constraint, with units unable to spend the time necessary to provide detailed information; a knowledge constraint, with units uncertain as to which KSAOs are appropriate; or a preference constraint, with units preferring a high overall level of performance compared with officers with specialized KSAOs. The lack of detailed knowledge about unit requirements has existed since an early pilot program (Rostker, 2015, p. 3).

Navy Perspective

The Navy experts stated that their service manages by performance, rather than a KSAO focus such as that seen in the Army. The Navy's talent management system supports a definition of talent as general ability. There is not necessarily a service standard on how to conduct talent management per se, but the experts agreed that the focus is on performance and the fulfillment of operational requirements.

That is not to say that the Navy ignores KSAOs entirely. The Navy experts noted that the service attempts to reuse certain skills multiple times in a career. Examples discussed in the interview included foreign language ability, particularly for those serving as FAOs. In that case, prospective FAOs receive language training that supports their first assignment as a FAO. Later in their careers, the service may align FAOs with a requirement that will again use that language training. The Navy experts also mentioned a similar process for graduates of the Naval Postgraduate School.[6]

The service may not fully appreciate all of the skills that individuals bring with them into the service, according to comments in the interview. However, the Navy experts pointed out that many of the required skills in the Navy have no analogue in the civilian world, such as "fighting a destroyer or fighting a jet."

Lastly, Navy experts highlighted that the up-or-out system limits their flexibility in talent management, echoing comments from our discussion on professional development. The sanction of involuntary separation from the military constrains officers to career time lines.

Air Force Perspective

Like the Navy, the Air Force manages its personnel with a focus on performance. We discussed how assignment officers have many of the tools that they need to make informed talent management decisions, including secretary-level reflections on promotion board results. There is a sense that the impact of talent management systems cannot substitute for an officer's overall performance; one interviewee stated that "the assignment officers cannot correct for several bad misses."

The Air Force experts mentioned that the Air Force may add additional rigor to its talent management systems. The Air Force would like to confirm whether the service is developing its people in the right way. Similarly, the Air Force is considering improving the tools available within its talent management system. To enhance the voice of both officers and gaining commanders in matching personnel to jobs, the Air Force has begun to implement an improved matching system that allows rank ordering of job openings by the officers vulnerable to move in an assignment cycle and rank ordering of the vulnerable officers by commanders with positions to fill. Assignment officers will broker the system to align the interests of officers and commanders to the extent possible.

---

[6] Previous RAND research evaluated the return on investment from graduate school education for naval officers. The research found that the return on investment substantially differed between surface warfare officers and meteorology and oceanography officers, largely explained by the differing likelihood of serving one or more tours in billets that require graduate education (Kamarck et al., 2010, p. 57).

Marine Corps Perspective

According to Marine Corps experts, the Marine Corps defines talent as the ability to succeed in one's tasks at the current and future ranks. The assignment process in the talent management system features face-to-face discussions between officers to be assigned and monitors who makes assignment decisions. The monitors are well versed in both the needs of an individual officer and the Marine Corps's standard professional development model.

The Marine Corps has discussed KSAOs for years, but in a different context from that of the Army. KSAOs, based on our discussion, boil down to "MOS credibility" and the ability to succeed in one's job. The important skill sets are those that translate into MOS requirements, rather than skills that exist outside an MOS. As a result, the Marine Corps experts highlighted that promotion board instructions that request an increase in a certain skill set are really asking for an increase in a particular MOS. The Marine Corps experts also noted that existing authorities in DOPMA and ROPMA allow the Marine Corps to manage talent effectively.

Conclusions

The services have wide latitude in talent management, and that latitude manifests in alternative approaches to the definition of talent. While the concept of talent evolves in some circumstances, the services rely on requirements to drive talent management. To some extent, broadening is a career luxury, as operational requirements are prioritized ahead of it.

Requirements drive the assignment process and similarly influence professional development models. An area for future study is how the military can account for low-density requirements that rely on softer skills that are more difficult to quantify.

Reporting Requirement: An Analysis of How Best to Encourage and Facilitate the Recruitment and Retention of Officers with Technical Expertise

Background

Technical expertise as a term is subject to many interpretations. It could refer to cyber or computer science expertise, and the RAND research team assumed that the use of the term included cyber. But technical expertise could also include other advanced technologies beyond cyber, such as artificial intelligence, data analytics, or advanced lasers and radars. Thus, we approached our interviews and analysis with the perspective that technical expertise includes cyber and other advanced technologies.

Technical expertise can include other technical domains beyond cyberlike fields, however. A case could be made that medical expertise is a form of technical expertise. A similar case could be made in a field like engineering—where there is a wide gap between an entry-level engineering degree and licensure as a professional engineer. The services' experience in addressing requirements in these fields informed our interviews.

Recent RAND studies addressed the barriers to recruiting a cyber workforce. Paul, Porche, and Axelband (2014, p. 46) compared the military's experience in establishing U.S. Special Operations Command with the emergence of cyber as a force. Whereas the special operations community recruits the majority of its force from the services, "[t]he cyber force needs nontraditional personnel authorities" (p. 46). The authors find that the skills needed for the cyber force are unlikely to be found within the military. To compensate for the shortfall, the authors recommend approaching recruitment as the military services do for medical professionals.

Overall, military compensation compares very favorably with civilian compensation, taking age and level of education into account (Hosek, Asch, and Mattock, 2012). At most stages, military members were found to be at or above the seventieth percentile of civilian wages. One area that could draw further attention, however, is compensation of recent college graduates who attended graduate school immediately after their undergraduate education, which was below the seventieth percentile in 2009. According to Hosek, Asch, and Mattock (2012, p. 15), "This finding may merit further attention, depending on whether the services find the supply and quality of junior officers to be adequate."

Themes

RAND researchers discussed the recruitment and retention of technical expertise with service representatives. Several themes emerged from the discussion.

Technical Expertise Recruitment Would Benefit from Increased Flexibility in Offering Constructive Credit

The service representatives all prefer expanded flexibility to offer constructive credit for those possessing technical expertise, which would grant time in service to new officers beyond the law's current three-year limitation. See the discussion of tenure management in Chapter Three.

The Definition of Technical Expertise Matters Somewhat—Generally Seen as Cyber Plus Other Advanced Fields

In our discussions, the service representatives agreed that technical expertise includes cyber skills. The service representatives also included other advanced fields in the realm of technical expertise, but the precise fields differed by service.

Technical Expertise Is Seen as One Facet of an Officer's Performance, but Not an Overarching Characteristic

The service representatives generally viewed technical expertise as an important skill set in some career fields but also emphasized a holistic approach to evaluating officers.

Existing Authorities Provide Retention Tools

Under existing authorities, the services possess numerous monetary and nonmonetary retention tools that can be applied to officers with technical expertise. Those authorities include monetary incentives such as bonuses, retention incentives, and special duty payments. Nonmonetary incentives include opportunities for specific postings or the opportunity to attend a civilian graduate school.

Army Perspective

Army experts drew parallels between technical expertise within the cyber field and expertise in other technically sophisticated areas, such as medicine and engineering. The Army experts merged those fields into the technical expertise bin based on the shared characteristics of advanced knowledge derived in part from civilian sources. Drawing on its experience with engineering and medicine, the Army will rely on the identification of requirements to determine the right level and type of technical expertise. The Army experts also included other emerging fields, such as artificial intelligence, under the auspices of technical expertise.

As with the other services, the Army desires increased flexibility to offer more than three years of constructive credit to potential officers with desired technical expertise.

Navy Perspective

Navy experts strongly supported increasing flexibility for recruiting individuals with technical expertise. They approached technical expertise as a range of emerging technologies, such as artificial intelligence, data analytics, or advanced lasers and radar. The experts viewed increased flexibility, such as the ability to offer more constructive credit, as a key recruiting tool. They emphasized that expanded authority granted now would allow the Navy to adapt to technological evolutions in the future, whatever it may be. Expanded authority would increase the talent pool beyond those the Navy can traditionally recruit and access as O-1s.

Air Force Perspective

Air Force experts noted that the Air Force is in competition with the private sector, and "getting at the high end of the bell curve is very challenging," as one expert put it. Recruiting individuals from premier technology schools could become very expensive and thus cannot be done too broadly. However, the Air Force experts pointed out that the service already recruits, through the U.S. Air Force Academy and ROTC, from the upper tiers of high school graduates.

The Air Force focus is on STEM degrees. The curriculum at the academy incorporates many STEM topics, making all officers at least "STEM aware," according to one expert. Overall, the Air Force experts felt that additional flexibility in awarding constructive credit would give them another option for competing for technical expertise.

Marine Corps Perspective

While the other services were considering recruiting technical expertise from the civilian world, the Marine Corps selected officers for cyber assignments from within the Marine Corps and based on unique methodology. According to the Marine Corps experts interviewed, the Marines saw value to bringing a "warfighting" mind-set to cyber assignments. The Marines saw less utility to a focus on technical expertise, particularly regarding cyber, and instead emphasize leadership qualities. Officers selected for cyber assignments typically come from related career fields, such as intelligence, communications, or targeting, so they do bring some familiarity with technical topics to a cyber assignment. The Marine Corps experts saw the warrant officer community as a natural location for technical expertise, rather than in their commissioned officers.

The Marine Corps experts also noted that the Marine Corps does not operate laboratories or as many specialized units, placing its role in technical expertise in a different light from that of the other services.

Conclusions

Technical expertise applies to an ever-changing compendium of skills, but insights into the acquisition and retention of cyber expertise can apply to emerging areas. The services see changes to constructive credit as an important recruitment tool. Not mentioned in any interview session was whether any cultural factors may make the recruitment and retention of those with cyber expertise a challenge, and thus this could be an area for future study.

CHAPTER FIVE

Active/Reserve Permeability

One topic pertained to active/reserve component permeability:[1] the utility and feasibility of allowing officers to transition repeatedly and seamlessly between active duty and reserve active-status throughout the course of their military careers.

As the services face critical personnel shortages in key specialties such as aviation, cyber, and intelligence, they are searching for innovative means to recruit and retain personnel by increasing the ability to transition seamlessly between the active component and reserve component. This type of permeability could enable more flexible career paths for service members. However, as our findings in this chapter indicate, some services are cautious about permeability—especially in light of the fact that the current promotion system does not reward cross-component experience.

Reporting Requirement: An Analysis of the Utility and Feasibility of Allowing Officers to Transition Repeatedly and Seamlessly Between Active Duty and Reserve Active-Status Throughout the Course of Their Military Careers

While our findings indicate that the service representatives perceive there to be several benefits associated with allowing officers to transition repeatedly and seamlessly between active duty and reserve active-status throughout the course of their military careers, there are also many barriers to such transitions. In addition, some representatives from the services indicated confusion about the ultimate goal of facilitating such seamless transitions, with some asking questions such as, "What are we trying to get to?"

In addition to service perspectives, we also sought and obtained National Guard perspectives on this issue. For each, we address the following topics: (1) the benefits of permeability, (2) the barriers to permeability, and (3) concerns regarding the current

---

[1] As defined by the NDAA reporting requirement, *permeability* refers to a service member's ability to transition seamlessly between active duty and reserve active-status during his or her military career.

scrolling process through which service members are moved to and from the active-duty list (ADL) and the reserve active-status list (RASL).[2]

Army Perspective

The Army has placed most of its combat support assets in its reserve components; thus, it has also linked its reserve components to the Regular Army. The Army has a history of experimenting with multicomponent units and currently has several pilot programs underway to provide officers with cross-component experiences.

Benefits of Permeability

Army representatives indicated to us that permeability has several benefits, including facilitating more flexible and different career paths for service members and potentially cutting down on the time it takes for service members to transition from their military careers to civilian careers when they separate from the military. In addition, Army representatives agreed that there is "an absolute need for some officers to have experiences in both the active and reserve component." However, despite these benefits, some Army representatives also asked, "What is the goal of permeability; what are we trying to get to with permeability?" The desired end state associated with permeability remains unclear to some; therefore, it is difficult to identify policy and legal changes that may be required to implement greater active component/reserve component permeability.

Barriers to Permeability

Army representatives identified many barriers to permeability. These barriers include legal constraints (e.g., shifting between Title 10 and Title 32 authorities, navigating reserve component duty statuses), cultural issues (e.g., the components not understanding each other), and administrative hurdles (e.g., disruptions in pay and benefits when shifting from one component to another; active and reserve systems not speaking to each other; a lack of information about position openings across the components). Army representatives also acknowledged that cultural changes will take place slowly; however, cross-component assignments (i.e., in which an active-component officer takes an assignment in a reserve-component unit or vice versa) could be incentivized by making them a requirement like joint assignments are currently, or by charging promotion boards to reward such cross-component experience.

Concerns with Scrolling

The Army experts cited the process of scrolling appointments between the ADL and the RASL as the most problematic barrier to permeability. They indicated very strongly

---

[2]   Scrolling is the process of preparing a list of officers for original appointment or reappointment by the Secretary of Defense or the President or confirmation by the Senate in a new grade, component, or, in some cases, corps.

that the current scrolling process consumes a great deal of time and resources, and that it should be automated. As one interviewee noted, the current scrolling process is "a paper process in an electronic world." For instance, it mandates that when appointments require White House or Senate approval, the services must send the White House and Senate hard copies of those appointment lists.

There is some concern in the Army that because it takes weeks, if not months, to complete the current scrolling process and finalize appointments, a lot of idle or unproductive time has been introduced into an officer's career as he or she waits to be scrolled from one list to another. The perceived end result is that officers have less productive time in appointments during their careers, and the Army has less time to grow and manage talent across the Army. There is also a perception in the Army that the scrolling process is having a negative impact on reserve-unit affiliation of officers leaving active duty; however, no data were cited during our discussions with Army representatives.

Army representatives indicated that they were in favor of moving toward a single, original appointment to the Army (rather than to an Army component), and that they were in favor of the development of a single scroll, as long as the Army could continue to manage cohorts in competitive categories across the components.[3]

Navy Perspective

Given that there is little overlap in the force structure and the equipping of the Navy Reserve and the active-component Navy, the Navy representatives we spoke with indicated that there is little movement of personnel across the components, except in specialty career paths such as force protection, the medical and dental corps, and the civil engineer corps. In fact, officers are discouraged from pursuing cross-component assignments.

Benefits of Permeability

Navy representatives indicated to us that there are some benefits to permeability. Most importantly, permeability provides a way to recruit and retain members of younger generations who want more flexibility in their career paths.

Barriers to Permeability

Navy representatives also identified several barriers to permeability. These include the mechanics of the current scrolling process, cultural barriers, and the current lack of integrated pay and personnel systems. Navy representatives told us that having inte-

---

[3] Currently, regular and reserve officers are separately scrolled, meaning that an officer moving from one component to the other must vacate the appointment in the losing component and be reappointed in the gaining component. Separate scrolling of active and reserve officers is required under terms contained in 10 U.S.C. If appointments were not component specific, scrolling would be required only for original appointments and promotions.

grated systems is a must in order to have permeability. While there are some policy issues, most of the barriers to permeability are associated with execution and the need for active and reserve systems to work together better than they currently do.

Concerns with Scrolling

The Navy also indicated that one of the biggest barriers to permeability is the current appointment scrolling process. The Navy representatives we spoke with indicated that the process is "very paper intensive" and an "administrative nightmare." When the appointment scrolls are sent to the Office of the Secretary of Defense, it takes four to six weeks to receive final approval because the office must ask the services clarifying questions regarding the individuals on the scrolls.

The Navy experts strongly recommended that the process be programmed or automated to avoid user errors and delays. In addition, they recommended trying to get some consensus across the services that original appointments should be made into a service, rather than a component. The Navy experts also agreed with the principle of a single appointment list.

Air Force Perspective

The Air Force has made a very deliberate decision to place key equipment and assets into the reserve components, thus ensuring that the Regular Air Force and the Air Reserve Component will be integrated. As a result, the Air Force is one of the most integrated services in terms of equipment and personnel.

Benefits of Permeability

The Air Force representatives we spoke with indicated that cross-component permeability allows the services to widen the options available to service members when they leave the active component, and it provides more links from the active component to the Guard and Reserve. Permeability also potentially facilitates increased utilization of the reserve component since there is a segment of the population who would not consider a full-time position in the military, but they would consider serving part time. The Air Force also sees permeability as a particularly promising tool for recruiting and retaining personnel in specialties where the Air Force is competing with high-paying civilian jobs (e.g., cyber, pilots). Lastly, the Air Force representatives we spoke with also indicated that they thought that training pipelines would benefit if total force career development and cross-component experience increased.

Barriers to Permeability

However, the Air Force representatives that we spoke with also indicated that there are several barriers to permeability. These include (1) problems with the current scrolling process, (2) the fact that the components have their own separation and reenlistment processes, and (3) the fact that there is little information disseminated regarding open vacancies across the components.

Concerns with Scrolling

The Air Force also cited the process of scrolling individuals between the ADL and the RASL as one of the most problematic barriers to permeability. The Air Force strongly supports a single appointment list; therefore, it would like to see officers commissioned into a service rather than into a particular component within a service.

Marine Corps Perspective

The Marine Corps's active and reserve components are among the most integrated of the services. For instance, each unit's table of organization and equipment is integrated across components, with 40 percent of each unit composed of personnel from the Selected Marine Corps Reserve, and 60 percent of each unit composed of personnel from the active component, active reserve program (Navy full-time support personnel and AGR personnel). The Marine Corps also has inspector-instructor duty, in which active component and active reserve Marines instruct and assist Selected Marine Corps Reserve units so that they can maintain readiness in those units. It is within this context that we asked Marine Corps representatives about the benefits and barriers to permeability, as well as potential ways to reduce problems associated with the current scrolling process.

Benefits of Permeability

Marine Corps representatives we spoke with indicated that while permeability could bring increased civilian experience and knowledge to the Marine Corps, they are not sure what other benefits permeability might have for the Marine Corps. They acknowledged that permeability could benefit individuals who may have a desire to move across the active and reserve components, but they felt that ultimately, the Marine Corps should manage movement across the components based on need, not individuals' desires.

These Marine Corps representatives also raised concerns that permeability can cause gaps in an officer's professional development that could cause the officer to fall behind his or her peer group. They felt that there needs to be more acknowledgment that currently, when Marines move from one component and another, they cannot simply rejoin their original component without potentially negative consequences. There are two sets of standards for reserve and active officers, and the perception is that permeability can have a negative impact on whether individuals can meet those standards after moving from one component to another.

Some Marine Corps representatives also indicated that the Marine Corps already has some mechanisms in place that facilitate movement across the components. These mechanisms include the return-to-active-duty boards (which identify critical MOSs in which the Marine Corps will allow reserve component members to return to active duty from prior service).

Barriers to Permeability

Marine Corps representatives also identified barriers to permeability. These barriers include scrolling from one component to another, as well as legal constraints on the use of the reserve component (including duty statuses). Since the representatives we spoke with said that the Marine Corps Reserve should be employed as a "gap filler, not a requirements filler," they indicated that some of these constraints are "good constraints" because too much reliance on the reserve components to fill operational requirements can deincentivize active-component force planning and requirements development. The Marine Corps representatives also indicated that it is unclear what the impact of the BRS may have on incentivizing (or deincentivizing) reserve-component members to come on active duty.

Concerns with Scrolling

The current scrolling process is problematic for the Marine Corps, but less so than for the other services. Marine Corps representatives indicated that while scrolling remains a drain on resources and time, it has gotten better. For instance, it used to take six to nine months to scroll someone between the ADL and RASL. It now takes two months. The Marine Corps representatives we spoke with also indicated that the Marine Corps already scrolls every active-component officer who can legally hold a reserve commission; therefore, this saves time if and when that officer takes a reserve commission.

Marine Corps representatives indicated to us that while they are in theory in favor of a single appointment list, they are concerned about the potential second- and third-order effects of such a change. They indicated that in order for the Marine Corps to support such a change, it would need to retain the flexibility to be able to manage competitive categories by component, as well as the ability to manage personnel who are now in three categories: the ADL, part-time reservists on the RASL, and full-time reservists on the RASL (Marines in the active reserve program, which includes Navy full-time support and AGR personnel).

National Guard Perspective

Since the National Guard operates under different statutory authorities from the other components, we also spoke with representatives from the ARNG and the ANG about the benefits of permeability, the barriers to permeability, and any suggestions they may have to address concerns with the current scrolling process.

Benefits of Permeability

Representatives from the ARNG indicated that increased permeability would allow officers to pursue different opportunities, families would also benefit from increased flexibilities, and ultimately it would help retain more service members.

ANG representatives indicated that one of the main benefits of permeability is that it enables a more flexible lifestyle and career path by allowing service members to serve part time at various points in their careers.

Barriers to Permeability

ARNG representatives also identified several barriers to permeability. For instance, they raised concerns that permeability could potentially hurt unit readiness when individuals flow out of units, and that there may be some gamesmanship of the system if easily repeated changes across components are allowed. In addition, some representatives raised concerns about how units might engage with individuals when they know that those individuals will be returning to their original component.

ARNG representatives also cautioned that career management does not currently occur across states. For instance, they indicated that it is difficult to identify unit vacancies in the ARNG, particularly since some state adjutants general do not want vacancies to be widely advertised and some commanders require that candidates interview for assignments.

In addition, they identified some legal barriers, including the fact that in order for an active officer to accept a state commission, the officer must first terminate his or her regular appointment. In addition, a state adjutant general can reject a service member from service in his or her state's National Guard.

ANG representatives indicated that a barrier to permeability is the way the current promotion system does not reward cross-component experience. In fact, such experience is often perceived as being detrimental to an officer's prospects for promotion, although this can vary by state.

Concerns with Scrolling

ARNG and ANG representatives recommended that the approval process be streamlined in the current scrolling process. For instance, there are multiple offices that must vet the appointment lists.

Conclusions

Our findings indicate that the service representatives agree that there are benefits to permeability—including the potential to recruit and retain individuals who are seeking more flexible career paths. However, representatives from the services also identified several barriers to permeability, including cultural, legal, and policy barriers. There was consensus among the service representatives that the current scrolling process is one of the biggest barriers to permeability. In considering options for improving the current scrolling process, there seems to be support for a single type of appointment to a service instead of a component. There is also support for a single appointment list,

Table 5.1
Service-Specific Recommendations for Improving Scrolling Process

Service	Recommendations for Improving Scrolling	Comments
Army	• Arrive at some consensus that an appointment is made to a service, not a component.	• Two separate lists serve to manage components, but a single list may be acceptable if components could continue to be managed separately.
Navy	• Automate the process. • Arrive at some consensus that an appointment is made to a service, not a component. • Develop a single list.	
Air Force	• Develop a single scroll. • Arrive at some consensus that an appointment is made to a service, not a component. • Clarify statutory piece of scrolling.	
Marine Corps	• Scroll everyone: every single officer who can legally hold a reserve commission. • A single list would be acceptable, as long as the services have flexibility to track and manage their officers. • Competitive promotion categories need to be preserved with a single list.	• In theory, representatives found a single list acceptable, but they were concerned about second- and third-order effects (e.g., breaking out individuals by promotion category by component).
ANG and ARNG	• Reduce coordination requirements for scrolls.	

as long as the services retain flexibility to manage competitive promotion categories by component. Table 5.1 summarizes the service-specific recommendations for improving the scrolling process.

CHAPTER SIX

Crosscutting Issues

Three NDAA reporting requirements cut across all of the bins identified in the previous chapters. These are

- an analysis of what actions have been or could be taken within current statutory authority to address officer management challenges
- an analysis of what actions can be taken by the armed forces to change the institutional culture regarding commonly held perceptions on appropriate promotion time lines, career progression, and traditional career paths
- an analysis of the impact that increased flexibility in promotion, assignments, and career length would have on officer competency in their MOSs.

Reporting Requirement: An Analysis of What Actions Have Been or Could Be Taken Within Current Statutory Authority to Address Officer Management Challenges

As discussed in Chapter Three, creation of new competitive categories for low-density or other specialized military occupations is clearly within the current authority of service secretaries. The Navy has used this authority to create a diversified set of competitive categories. The Army and the Air Force are contemplating creation of additional categories.

Also highlighted in Chapter Three is the Marine Corps's use of career designation boards at the O-3 level to provide early force shaping. By eliminating lower-quality officers early in their careers, it minimizes developmental investment in officers who would otherwise be involuntarily separated at a midcareer point.

As discussed in Chapter Four, the services have used selective continuation authorities to temper the fundamental up-or-out characteristics of the officer promotion system. This authority has been used when it meets retention needs and when the retained officers are fully qualified for service in their current grade. However, due to the negative connotation associated with characterizing these officers as having "failed of selection for promotion," it provides a less-than-ideal approach for those whose continued service is needed and valued.

As discussed in Chapter Five, the services are in some cases moving toward talent management approaches that afford greater attention to KSAOs of individual officers or that give officers and commanders more meaningful voice in assignment actions. Greater exploitation of emerging technology makes this possible.

Reporting Requirement: An Analysis of What Actions Can Be Taken by the Armed Forces to Change the Institutional Culture Regarding Commonly Held Perceptions on Appropriate Promotion Time Lines, Career Progression, and Traditional Career Paths

As discussed in Chapters Two, Three, and Four, institutional cultures still favor the conventional DOPMA/ROPMA framework for meeting most officer requirements, particularly for core warfighting occupations. If a cultural shift is needed, it would be better to accommodate low-density occupations or specific requirements in which development and utilization patterns differ from the norm. For services that have retained broadly defined competitive categories for promotion of their line officers, a shift toward more differentiated categories to meet these needs would entail in itself a cultural shift at the institutional level. Willingness to move in this direction is evident.

The service representatives we spoke with generally expressed a need to tie development, particularly advanced education or career broadening, to requirements. Moreover, they tended to see a need for an *immediate* requirement to justify the investment.[1] Such an attitude is most visible in the approach to advanced education, where postschooling utilization draws on the skills learned in graduate school. A longer view of requirements, such as the need for informed strategic leadership in the future, might lead to the creation of early development opportunities that lay the foundation for longer-term needs. A longer view of requirements may also create more flexibility for the services to respond to changes in the environment. A bench of broadened officers today could provide a more diverse and arguably better-suited pool of future senior leaders for the challenges of the next decade, whatever they may be.

The services also approach requirements from a centrally managed perspective. Through bureaucratic management and centralized validation, services identify a need and commit resources to satisfy the requirement. The requirement originator, often a command, loses ownership of the process through which the requirement is met. Anna Simons explained this challenge as it related to the Army, where a need for experienced

---

[1]   We note that DoD policy does not specify an immediate requirement. It requires that graduate education programs meet "a present need, anticipated requirement, or future capability" (DoDI 1322.10, p. 2).

soldiers in advisory missions was fulfilled by sending inexperienced soldiers. Commanders did not have the authority to choose the experience level or background of those who would serve in the role (Simons, 2017, pp. 16–18). While the services centrally validate, track, and satisfy requirements today, modern information technology platforms could pass that responsibility to commanders and provide them ownership of their requirements.

Chapter Four includes a discussion of how the composition of promotion boards tends to prolong existing perspectives regarding the relative value of various career paths. Service secretaries can signal support for highly valued but unconventional paths through the selection of officers with certain backgrounds to serve on boards, through their instructions to boards, and of course by establishing competitive categories that help to avoid the challenge of weighing the relative merits of conventional and unconventional career paths.

As discussed in Chapter Five, cultural differences between the active and reserve components to some degree reinforce the limited permeability between the components. While the flow of officers from the active to the reserve component is common and highly valued, flow in the opposite direction is uncommon and, with some exceptions, the active components do not have processes in place to encourage or support the flow of officers from the reserve components.[2] That flow would be enhanced by building the necessary support structures, including routine identification of assignments with needs for experienced officers and standing procedures for receiving and processing requests from reserve officers to fill those needs. As the flow of reserve officers to the active components increased, cultural resistance to that flow might attenuate.

In the long run, the use of separate active and reserve chains of command starting from the highest organizational levels, as is the practice for Army and Air Force components, reinforces cultural gaps between the components. Anything that can be done to reduce these organizational divisions would almost certainly lead to greater permeability and, more importantly, better utilization of forces.

Reporting Requirement: An Analysis of the Impact That Increased Flexibility in Promotion, Assignments, and Career Length Would Have on Officer Competency in Their Military Occupational Specialties

The services generally saw conventional authorities and policies as well suited to the development of required competencies in core MOSs—those most directly involved in warfighting functions. As discussed throughout Chapters Two, Three, and Four,

---

[2]   The comments here refer to reappointment of officers in a different component. They do not pertain to activation of reserve units or individuals to meet active mission needs.

increased flexibilities were seen as most useful in developing depth in technical specialties for which training, education, and experience requirements may not align well with conventional authorities and policies.

CHAPTER SEVEN

Flexibilities Introduced in the 2019 National Defense Authorization Act

Background

On August 13, 2018, President Donald Trump signed the John S. McCain National Defense Authorization Act for Fiscal Year 2019 into law. The FY 2019 NDAA addresses many of the issues laid forth in the reporting requirements articulated in the FY 2018 NDAA and presented in the previous chapters. This chapter describes each provision in Title V (Military Personnel Policy), Subtitle A (Officer Personnel Policy), Sections 501–507. The chapter further provides analysis on how each provision evolves larger efforts to modernize officer management.

Specific Provisions

Section 501

Repeal of requirement for ability to complete 20 years of service by age 62 as qualification for original appointment as a regular commissioned officer.

Section 501 of the FY 2019 NDAA amends Section 532, 10 U.S.C. Previously, the law established that all officers must be able to complete 20 years of service by age 62 at the time of commissioning.[1] While intended to maintain a "young and vigorous force," the age restriction limited the recruitment pool to those individuals 42 years or younger, potentially restricting the services' access to critical skills and industry experience. Section 501 lifts the age restriction, opening the recruitment aperture to a larger pool of candidates. While the reform enables the services to target specific technical expertise, it is broad enough to apply to any critical skill set. In combination with Section 502 (see the next section), it may enable the services to commission more experienced officers at higher pay grades.

---

[1]   The requirement to retire by age 62 remains.

Section 502

Enhancement of availability of constructive service credit for private-sector training or experience upon original appointment as a commissioned officer.

Section 502 of the FY 2019 NDAA amends Subsection (b), Section 533, 10 U.S.C. (for active-duty officers) and Subsection (b), Section 12207, 10 U.S.C. (for reserve officers). Before the FY 2019 NDAA, constructive service credit for private-sector training was capped at the amount required for original appointment in the grade of O-4. Additionally, constructive credit was reserved for the medical and dental corps. Section 502 allows for constructive credit required for original appointment up to the grade of O-6 and removes restrictions on career fields. The new language delegates authority to the service secretaries to designate additional credit if the secretary deems that an officer's training or experience directly meets an operational need for his or her service. The increased grade flexibility will enable the services to offer more competitive rank and compensation to individuals with critical skill sets in order to meet service needs.

Section 503

Standardized temporary promotion authority across the military departments for officers in certain grades with critical skills.

Section 503 of the FY 2019 NDAA updates Section 605, Chapter 35, 10 U.S.C. This section delegates authority to the service secretary to standardize temporary promotions for officers serving in a position requiring a grade increase. Temporary promotions may enable the services to fill critical skill sets quickly and provide retention incentives for highly competent individuals.

In order for an officer to receive a temporary promotion, he or she must have a specific skill that is in a critical shortage, as determined by the service secretary. The temporary promotion does not change the officer's position on the ADL. A temporary promotion board must convene and select an officer for a temporary promotion. While serving under the temporary promotion authority, the officer is entitled to the pay and allowances of the grade of the temporary promotion. The temporary promotion is considered terminated when the individual is promoted through a regular promotion board, or when the individual is no longer serving in the position requiring the rank. The law limits the number of temporary promotions by service as follows (Table 7.1).

Section 504

Authority for promotion boards to recommend officers of particular merit be placed higher on a promotion list.

Section 504 of the FY 2019 NDAA amends Sections 616 and 617, 10 U.S.C. Previously, the sequence of officers on promotion lists was determined by time in grade.

Table 7.1
Limitation on the Number of Temporary Promotions

Service and Rank	Number of Temporary Promotions
Army	
Captain	120
Major	350
Lieutenant colonel	200
Colonel	100
Air Force	
Captain	100
Major	325
Lieutenant colonel	175
Colonel	80
Marine Corps	
Captain	50
Major	175
Lieutenant colonel	100
Colonel	50
Navy	
Lieutenant	100
Lieutenant commander	325
Commander	175
Captain	80

Under the new provision, selection boards may recommend officers of particular merit to be placed higher on the promotion list. In order to be placed higher based on merit, an officer must receive the recommendation of at least the majority of the board members unless a service secretary establishes an alternate requirement. The service secretary must authorize the use of a merit-based promotion list.

Some officers have articulated, through surveys, dissatisfaction with the current promotion system, which is based on time in grade. Merit-based promotion sequencing may assuage some officers' dissatisfaction, rewarding superior performance with the incentive of earlier promotion.

Section 505

Authority for officers to opt out of promotion board consideration.

Section 505 of the FY 2019 NDAA amends Section 619, 10 U.S.C. (for active-duty officers) and Section 14301, 10 U.S.C. (for reserve officers). The provision delegates authority to the service secretaries to approve officers' requests to opt out of a promotion board. The secretary may approve an officer's opt-out request if the basis for the request is to allow an officer to complete a broadening assignment, advanced education, another assignment of significant value to the department, or a career progression requirement delayed by the assignment or education. Further, the secretary must determine that the delayed promotion is in the interest of the department. The provision further states that officers are eligible to opt out of promotion only if they have not previously been passed over for selection.

Section 506

Applicability to additional officer grades of authority for continuation on active duty of officers in certain military specialties and career tracks.

Section 506 of the FY 2019 NDAA amends Section 637a(a), 10 U.S.C. Previously, service members could not be considered for selective continuation in grade after being twice passed over for promotion until they attained the grade of O-4. This provision adjusts eligibility for selective continuation to the grade of O-2.

Section 507

Alternative promotion authority for officers in designated competitive categories of officers.

Section 507 of the FY 2019 NDAA amends Section 649, 10 U.S.C. The provision delegates authority to the service secretaries to designate one or more competitive categories with the authority for alternative promotion paths. In order to establish a new competitive category, a service secretary must submit a report to Congress 60 days before utilizing the new competitive category. In the report, the service secretary must provide a description of officer requirements for officers within the category, the number of opportunities for consideration for promotion to each grade and an estimate of promotion timing within the category, and an estimate of the size of the promotion zone (the number of years of eligibility for promotion), not to exceed five years.

Under the alternate promotion authority, standard tenure management considerations do not apply. Within a competitive category, there are no BPZ or APZ promotions. Time-in-grade requirements do not apply within a competitive category under the alternative promotion authority. However, a selection board for the competitive category may recommend that an officer be excluded from future considerations for promotion. If the secretary of the military department reduces the number of opportunities for promotion consideration, an officer within the competitive category will be afforded one more opportunity for consideration after the reduction. An officer is not considered "twice deferred" until nonselected on the last of this series of considerations. In that event, the officer may be selectively continued.

The new authority provides pathways for technical-track careers, such as the Air Force "fly-only" pilot track or a more technically focused cyber career. Under the new authority, these career paths would focus on developing and maintaining technical depth, with few or none of the broadening assignments and professional military education opportunities associated with the traditional leadership track. Further, the broad language used to establish the authority provides the service secretaries the flexibility to target specific career fields or grades as the need arises.

Relationship to Reporting Requirements in the 2018 National Defense Authorization Act

Table 7.2 shows how the new provisions in the 2019 NDAA are closely aligned with many of the exploratory reporting requirements contained in the 2018 NDAA.

Table 7.2
FY 2019 NDAA Provisions

FY 2018 NDAA Section 572 Reporting Requirement	2019 NDAA Section						
	501	502	503	504	505	506	507
Promotions							
Evaluation of the impact on officer retention of granting promotion boards the authority to recommend officers of particular merit be placed at the top of the promotion list				X			
An analysis of the reasons and frequency with which officers in the grade of O-3 or above are passed over for promotion to the next-highest grade, particularly those officers who have pursued advanced degrees, broadening assignments, and nontraditional career paths					X		
An analysis of the utility and feasibility of creating new competitive categories or an independent career and promotion path for officers in low-density MOSs							X
An analysis of how the armed forces can avoid an officer corps disproportionately weighted toward officers serving in the grades of major, lieutenant colonel, and colonel and Navy grades of lieutenant commander, commander, and captain, if statutory officer grade caps are relaxed							
Tenure							
A statistical analysis, based on exit surveys and other data available to the military departments, of the impact that current personnel policies under DOPMA have on the recruiting and retention of qualified regular and reserve officers in the armed forces—specifically, the statistical analysis shall include an estimate of the number of officers who leave the armed forces each year because of their dissatisfaction with the current personnel policies, including career progression, promotion policies, and a perceived lack of opportunity for schooling and broadening assignments			X	X	X		X
An analysis of the benefits and limitations of the current promotion time lines and the "up or out" system required by policy and law					X	X	X
An analysis of the utility and feasibility of encouraging officers to pursue careers of lengths that vary from the traditional 20-year military career and the mechanisms that could be employed to encourage officers to pursue these varying career lengths	X		X		X	X	X
An analysis of the current officer force–shaping authorities and any changes needed to these authorities to improve recruiting, retention, and readiness							
An analysis of any other matters the Secretary of Defense considers appropriate to improve the effective recruitment and retention of officers							

Table 7.2—Continued

FY 2018 NDAA Section 572 Reporting Requirement	2019 NDAA Section						
	501	502	503	504	505	506	507
Talent management							
An analysis of the extent to which current personnel policies inhibit the professional development of officers					X		
An analysis of the efficacy of officer talent management systems currently used by the military departments							
An analysis of how best to encourage and facilitate the recruitment and retention of officers with technical expertise	X	X	X		X		X
Active/reserve permeability							
An analysis of the utility and feasibility of allowing officers to transition repeatedly and seamlessly between active duty and reserve active-status throughout the course of their military careers							
Crosscutting issues							
An analysis of what actions have been or could be taken within current statutory authority to address officer management challenges							
An analysis of what actions can be taken by the armed forces to change the institutional culture regarding commonly held perceptions of appropriate promotion time lines, career progression, and traditional career paths							
An analysis of the impact that increased flexibility in promotion, assignments, and career length would have on officer competency in their MOSs				X	X	X	X

CHAPTER EIGHT

Conclusions and Recommendations

We reached several broad conclusions regarding officer career management and its relationship to DOPMA and ROPMA.

- The military departments believe that DOPMA and ROPMA continue to provide an effective overall framework for managing the careers of officers in core warfighting communities.
- Where change is needed, it is primarily to accommodate needs in low-density occupations, to foster the pursuit of unconventional but useful career paths, or to permit an earlier shift of more promising officers from tactical to strategic skill development.
- The services are more open now to new flexibilities in officer career management than they were when Secretary of Defense Ashton Carter's Force of the Future proposals were first unveiled.
- The one phenomenon that signals a need for new flexibilities more than any other is the employment of military personnel in offensive cyber warfare. There is a perception, not yet fully in focus, that conventional career management approaches may not yield the human capital needed for success in this mission set.

In our conversations with service representatives to gather their perspectives for this report, we found that openness to new officer career management flexibilities is married to a strong sense that implementation should be at the discretion of service secretaries. We sense a willingness to depart from the emphasis on standardization promulgated by DOPMA and ROPMA and shift toward greater differentiation of career and talent management approaches across the services and for different needs within each of the services. Secretarial discretion allows the services to tailor their approaches to specific needs and to allow gradual adoption of new flexibilities as their longer-range consequences become better understood.

While some of the officer management flexibilities emerging in recent and pending legislation represent definite departures from long-standing DOPMA and ROPMA provisions, we characterize this modernization trend as more incremental and evolutionary than the landmark officer management changes (DOPMA, ROPMA, and Goldwater-Nichols) that preceded it. We sense that all of the relevant stakeholders—congressional committees, Office of the Secretary of Defense and service leadership and personnel policy staffs, and individual officers—are comfortable with this approach.

Our recommendation to the services is to search for innovative ways to take advantage of existing and emerging flexibilities. Our recommendation to legislators is to provide service secretaries with the latitude to adapt innovatively to their current and future challenges.

Review and Reporting Topics

Table A.1 lists the review and reporting elements required by Section 572 of the FY 2018 NDAA. The elements were sorted into the topical bins shown in this table to facilitate their discussion and analysis.

Table A.1
Review and Reporting Issues by Topic

Topics	Issues
Promotions	
	Evaluation of the impact on officer retention of granting promotion boards the authority to recommend that officers of particular merit be placed at the top of the promotion list
	An analysis of the reasons and frequency with which officers in the grade of O-3 or above are passed over for promotion to the next-highest grade, particularly those officers who have pursued advanced degrees, broadening assignments, and nontraditional career paths
	An analysis of the utility and feasibility of creating new competitive categories or an independent career and promotion path for officers in low-density MOSs
	An analysis of how the armed forces can avoid an officer corps disproportionately weighted toward officers serving in the grades of major, lieutenant colonel, and colonel and Navy grades of lieutenant commander, commander, and captain, if statutory officer grade caps are relaxed
Tenure	
	A statistical analysis, based on exit surveys and other data available to the military departments, of the impact that current personnel policies under DOPMA have on recruiting and retention of qualified regular and reserve officers of the armed forces—specifically, the statistical analysis shall include an estimate of the number of officers who leave the armed forces each year because of dissatisfaction with the current personnel policies, including career progression, promotion policies, and a perceived lack of opportunity for schooling and broadening assignments
	An analysis of the benefits and limitations of the current promotion time lines and the "up-or-out" system required by policy and law
	An analysis of the utility and feasibility of encouraging officers to pursue careers of lengths that vary from the traditional 20-year military career and the mechanisms that could be employed to encourage officers to pursue these varying career lengths
	An analysis of the current officer force–shaping authorities and any changes needed to these authorities to improve recruiting, retention, and readiness
	An analysis of any other matters the Secretary of Defense considers appropriate to improve the effective recruitment and retention of officers
Talent management	
	An analysis of the extent to which current personnel policies inhibit the professional development of officers
	An analysis of the efficacy of officer talent management systems currently used by the military departments
	An analysis of how best to encourage and facilitate the recruitment and retention of officers with technical expertise
Active/reserve permeability	
	An analysis of the utility and feasibility of allowing officers to transition repeatedly and seamlessly between active duty and reserve active status throughout the course of their military careers

Table A.1—Continued

Topics	Issues

Crosscutting issues

An analysis of what actions have been or could be taken within current statutory authority to address officer management challenges

An analysis of what actions can be taken by the armed forces to change the institutional culture regarding commonly held perceptions on appropriate promotion time lines, career progression, and traditional career paths

An analysis of the impact that increased flexibility in promotion, assignments, and career length would have on officer competency in their MOSs

Selected Status of Forces Survey Results

Tables B.1–B.14 in this appendix provide response frequencies for selected items from the 2016 Status of Forces Survey fielded by the Defense Manpower Data Center. For some items, the response tabulations include "no response" (indicating that the respondent made it to that point in the survey but did not provide a response for that particular question) and "not on form" (indicating that the respondent stopped responding before reaching that item on the survey).

Active Duty

Table B.1
Item 108a: How Much Do You Agree or Disagree with the Statement, "I Will Get the Assignments I Need to Be Competitive for Promotion"?

	Grade						Total
	O-1	O-2	O-3	O-4	O-5	O-6 and above	
Strongly agree	33	45	182	119	89	64	532
Agree	93	162	469	291	174	93	1,282
Neither agree nor disagree	42	81	234	154	82	28	621
Disagree	13	43	130	95	60	20	361
Strongly disagree	5	15	52	40	22	3	137
Total responses	186	346	1,067	699	427	208	2,933
No response	29	56	163	67	32	10	357
Not on form	213	423	1,237	737	497	198	3,341

Table B.2
Item 108b: How Much Do You Agree or Disagree with the Statement, "My Service's Evaluation/Selection System Is Effective in Promoting Its Best Members"?

	Grade						Total
	O-1	O-2	O-3	O-4	O-5	O-6 and above	
Strongly agree	18	24	72	49	55	48	266
Agree	61	95	286	204	146	100	892
Neither agree nor disagree	55	96	235	142	99	24	651
Disagree	36	82	274	174	84	29	679
Strongly disagree	16	49	199	128	45	7	444
Total responses	186	346	1,066	697	429	208	2,932
No response	29	56	164	69	30	10	358
Not on form	213	423	1,273	737	497	198	3,341

Table B.3
Item 108c: How Much Do You Agree or Disagree with the Statement, "If I Stay in the Service, I Will Be Promoted as High as My Ability and Effort Warrant"?

	Grade						Total
	O-1	O-2	O-3	O-4	O-5	O-6 and above	
Strongly agree	30	38	174	93	68	61	464
Agree	89	148	372	242	147	74	1,072
Neither agree nor disagree	38	78	229	142	85	36	608
Disagree	19	56	186	134	86	34	515
Strongly disagree	10	23	105	87	41	3	269
Total responses	186	343	1,066	698	427	208	2,928
No response	29	59	164	68	32	10	362
Not on form	213	423	1,273	737	497	198	3,341

Table B.4
Item 109a: How Satisfied Are You with Your Level of Responsibility on the Job?

	Grade						Total
	O-1	O-2	O-3	O-4	O-5	O-6 and above	
Very satisfied	42	73	296	224	171	110	916
Satisfied	97	203	564	364	194	76	1,498
Neither satisfied nor dissatisfied	28	33	97	59	23	11	251
Dissatisfied	17	26	89	39	30	8	209
Very dissatisfied	2	8	22	12	9	2	55
Total responses	186	343	1,068	698	427	207	2,929
No response	29	59	162	68	32	11	361
Not on form	213	423	1,273	737	497	198	3,341

Table B.5
Item 109b: How Satisfied Are You with Your Level of Authority on the Job?

	Grade						Total
	O-1	O-2	O-3	O-4	O-5	O-6 and above	
Very satisfied	36	68	242	190	154	95	785
Satisfied	89	182	510	348	168	77	1,374
Neither satisfied nor dissatisfied	29	40	138	74	42	16	339
Dissatisfied	29	44	138	61	49	15	336
Very dissatisfied	3	9	37	21	13	4	87
Total responses	186	343	1,065	694	426	207	2,921
No response	29	59	165	72	33	11	369
Not on form	213	423	1,273	737	497	198	3,341

Table B.6
Item 109c: How Satisfied Are You with Your Opportunities for Promotion?

	Grade						Total
	O-1	O-2	O-3	O-4	O-5	O-6 and above	
Very satisfied	31	46	149	112	88	62	488
Satisfied	94	167	482	265	151	76	1,235
Neither satisfied nor dissatisfied	41	84	215	133	76	37	586
Dissatisfied	16	34	140	125	79	24	4,184
Very dissatisfied	4	12	81	63	32	8	200
Total responses	186	343	1,067	698	426	207	2,957
No response	29	59	163	88	33	11	383
Not on form	213	423	1,273	737	497	198	3,341

Table B.7
Item 109d: How Satisfied Are You with Your Chances to Acquire Valuable Job Skills?

	Grade						Total
	O-1	O-2	O-3	O-4	O-5	O-6 and above	
Very satisfied	49	64	228	161	126	89	717
Satisfied	94	169	502	333	192	89	1,379
Neither satisfied nor dissatisfied	27	55	185	115	68	22	472
Dissatisfied	10	39	116	69	31	3	268
Very dissatisfied	6	15	32	20	9	2	84
Total responses	186	342	1,063	698	426	205	2,920
No response	—	—	—	—	—	—	—

Table B.8
Item 20a: Taking All Things into Consideration, How Satisfied Are You, in General, with Your Total Compensation?

	Grade						Total
	O-1	O-2	O-3	O-4	O-5	O-6 and above	
Very satisfied	86	188	574	322	280	127	1,577
Satisfied	250	442	1,332	825	504	227	3,580
Neither satisfied nor dissatisfied	48	87	276	161	80	33	685
Dissatisfied	33	79	237	157	64	21	591
Very dissatisfied	5	15	52	25	13	4	114
Total responses	422	811	2,471	1,490	941	412	6,547
No response	6	14	32	13	15	4	84

Table B.9
Item 20b: Taking All Things into Consideration, How Satisfied Are You, in General, with the Type of Work You Do in Your Military Job?

	Grade						Total
	O-1	O-2	O-3	O-4	O-5	O-6 and above	
Very satisfied	112	168	635	422	334	181	1,852
Satisfied	192	370	1,165	760	447	178	3,112
Neither satisfied nor dissatisfied	64	113	326	145	80	25	753
Dissatisfied	37	117	241	118	55	21	589
Very dissatisfied	10	30	80	32	19	4	175
Total responses	428	825	2,503	1,503	956	416	6,631
No response	13	27	56	26	21	7	150

Table B.10
Item 20c: Taking All Things into Consideration, How Satisfied Are You, in General, with Your Opportunities for Promotion?

	Grade						Total
	O-1	O-2	O-3	O-4	O-5	O-6 and above	
Very satisfied	92	134	378	217	195	115	1,131
Satisfied	217	402	1,143	646	391	164	2,963
Neither satisfied nor dissatisfied	90	165	468	267	149	79	1,218
Dissatisfied	12	74	315	255	148	45	849
Very dissatisfied	6	26	147	98	57	11	345
Total responses	417	801	2,451	1,483	940	414	6,506
No response	11	24	52	20	16	2	125

Table B.11
Item 20d: Taking All Things into Consideration, How Satisfied Are You, in General, with the Quality of Your Coworkers?

	Grade						Total
	O-1	O-2	O-3	O-4	O-5	O-6 and above	
Very satisfied	116	135	530	351	290	166	1,588
Satisfied	202	409	1,212	799	485	190	3,297
Neither satisfied nor dissatisfied	63	149	456	211	104	33	1,016
Dissatisfied	30	100	192	94	46	18	480
Very dissatisfied	10	16	66	23	11	5	131
Total responses	421	809	2,456	1,478	936	412	6,512
No response	7	16	47	25	20	4	119

Table B.12
Item 20e: Taking All Things into Consideration, How Satisfied Are You, in General, with the Quality of Your Supervisor?

	Grade						Total
	O-1	O-2	O-3	O-4	O-5	O-6 and above	
Very satisfied	127	203	677	446	380	188	2,021
Satisfied	198	355	1,075	687	375	160	2,850
Neither satisfied nor dissatisfied	50	120	374	190	100	40	874
Dissatisfied	33	91	233	111	65	18	551
Very dissatisfied	11	38	107	54	24	7	241
Total responses	419	807	2,466	1,488	944	413	6,537
No response	9	18	37	15	12	3	94

Table B.13
Item 163: Suppose That You Have to Decide Whether to Stay on Active Duty. Which of the Following Would Be the Most Important Factor in Your Decision?

	Grade						Total
	O-1	O-2	O-3	O-4	O-5	O-6 and above	
Amount of personal and family time you have	12	21	58	39	21	7	158
Amount of time you spend away from home station	1	4	34	30	14	2	85
Child care	1	2	—	1	—	—	4
Choice of jobs	14	24	45	22	20	9	134
Dental insurance for your family	1	—	1	—	—	—	2
Family concerns	19	22	82	39	29	23	214
Family financial stability	8	12	49	34	16	7	126
Family support issues	2	1	6	2	1	1	13
Health care for family	2	5	11	9	11	2	40
Health care for you	2	1	5	1	4	1	14
Job security	9	22	46	18	4	3	102
Level of challenge in your job	3	4	18	14	7	6	52
Level of integrity in your unit	1	3	3	—	—	—	7
Military retirement system	10	25	141	166	66	14	422
Military values, lifestyle, and tradition	4	10	28	29	15	14	100
Off-duty education opportunities	2	1	2	1	—	—	6
Opportunities for career advancement	8	14	62	45	39	8	176
Opportunities for stabilized tours	1	1	29	14	6	2	53
Opportunities for training and professional development	4	13	32	6	10	2	67
Opportunities to be assigned to station of choice	4	30	59	26	33	7	159
Opportunities to travel	2	8	9	4	2	—	25
Opportunity for retraining	1	—	3	—	—	—	4
Other	2	7	31	11	11	3	65

Table B.13—Continued

	Grade						Total
	O-1	O-2	O-3	O-4	O-5	O-6 and above	
Pay and allowances	9	12	65	39	26	13	164
Personal choice/freedoms	13	33	83	21	21	8	179
Pride in serving your country	7	10	26	19	19	12	93
Quality of leadership	3	7	35	6	11	7	69
Quality of work environment	8	23	40	10	14	4	99
Recognition	1	—	1	—	—	—	2
Sense of accomplishment	10	27	54	34	19	9	153
Special pays/bonus programs	2	5	29	14	6	2	58
Spouse/family attitudes	9	11	61	35	34	20	170
Total	174	358	1,148	689	459	186	3,014

Reserve

Table B.14
Item 43: Suppose That You Have to Decide Whether to Continue to Participate in the National Guard/Reserve. Assuming You Could Stay, How Likely Is It That You Would Choose to Stay?

	Grade						Total
	O-1	O-2	O-3	O-4	O-5	O-6 and above	
Very likely	189	341	1,106	972	716	297	3,621
Likely	131	199	755	514	386	150	2,135
Neither likely nor unlikely	40	79	183	104	88	35	529
Unlikely	31	49	131	61	81	32	385
Very unlikely	16	39	56	42	42	13	208
Total responses	407	707	2,231	1,693	1,313	527	6,878
No response	6	7	28	15	7	1	64

Statutory and Policy Provisions by Topic

The following tables provide selected DOPMA and ROPMA statutory and policy provisions by topic, with corresponding DoD or service policy provisions. Table C.1 provides promotion-related topics, and Table C.2 provides tenure-related topics.

Table C.1
Promotion-Related Statutory and Policy Provisions by Topic

Topic	Statute	Policy
Regular—control grades 10 U.S.C. 523(a)(1)	Except as provided in subsection (c), of the total number of commissioned officers serving on active duty in the Army, Air Force, or Marine Corps at the end of any fiscal year (excluding officers in categories specified in subsection (b)), the number of officers who may be serving on active duty in each of the grades of major, lieutenant colonel, and colonel may not, as of the end of such fiscal year, exceed a number determined in accordance with the following table:	
Regular— exemptions 10 U.S.C. 523(b)	Officers in the following categories shall be excluded in computing and determining authorized strengths under this section: (1)Reserve officers— (A) on active duty as authorized under section 115(a)(1)(B) or 115(b)(1) of this title, or excluded from counting for active duty end strengths under section 115(i) of this title; (B) on active duty under section 10211, 10302 through 10305, or 12402 of this title or under section 708 of title 32; or (C) on full-time National Guard duty. (2) General and flag officers. (3) Medical officers. (4) Dental officers. (5) Warrant officers. (6) Retired officers on active duty under a call or order to active duty for 180 days or less. (7) Retired officers on active duty under section 10(b)(2) of the Military Selective Service Act (50 U.S.C. 3809(b)(2)) for the administration of the Selective Service System. (8) Permanent professors of the United States Military Academy and the United States Air Force Academy and professors of the United States Naval Academy who are career military professors (as defined in regulations prescribed by the Secretary of the Navy), but not to exceed 50 from any such academy. (9) Officers who are Senior Military Acquisition Advisors under section 1725 of this title, but not to exceed 15.	DoD I DoDI 6000.13 The authorized strengths of the Military Departments for HPOs [health professions officers] on active duty (AD) or in an active status in the RC [reserve component] in grades below brigadier general and rear admiral (lower half) will be based on the needs of the Military Departments. Those strengths will be determined by the Secretary of the Military Department concerned, in coordination with the Assistant Secretary of Defense for Health Affairs (ASD(HA)) and the Assistant Secretary of Defense for Manpower and Reserve Affairs (ASD(M&RA)).

Table C.1—Continued

Topic	Statute	Policy
Reserve—Army and Air Force control grades 10 U.S.C. 12005(a)(2)	A strength prescribed by the Secretary concerned under paragraph (1) for a grade may not be higher than the percentage of the strength authorized for the Army or the Air Force, as the case may be, under section 12003 of this title that is specified for that grade as follows:	

Grade	Army percentage	Air Force percentage
Colonel	2	1.8
Lieutenant colonel	6	4.6
Major	13	14.0
Captain	35	32.0
First lieutenant and second lieutenant (when combined with the number authorized for general officer grades under section 12004 of this title)	44	47

Topic	Statute	Policy
Reserve—Army and Air Force exemptions 10 U.S.C. 12005(a)(3)	Medical officers and dental officers shall not be counted for the purposes of this subsection.	

Table C.1—Continued

Topic	Statute	Policy
Reserve—Navy control grades 10 U.S.C. 12005(b)(1)	The authorized strengths of the Navy Reserve in line officers in an active status in the grades of captain, commander, lieutenant commander, and lieutenant, and in the grades of lieutenant (junior grade) and ensign combined, are the following percentages of the total authorized number of those officers:	

Captain	1.5 percent
Commander	7 percent
Lieutenant commander	22 percent
Lieutenant	37 percent
Lieutenant (junior grade) and ensign (when combined with the number authorized for flag officer grades under section 12004 of this title)	32.5 percent

Topic	Statute	Policy
Reserve—Marine Corps control grades 10 U.S.C. 12005(c)(1)	The authorized strengths of the Marine Corps Reserve in officers in an active status in the grades of colonel, lieutenant colonel, major, and captain, and in the grades of first lieutenant and second lieutenant combined, are the following percentages of the total authorized number of those officers:	

Colonel	2 percent
Lieutenant colonel	8 percent
Major	16 percent
Captain	39 percent
First lieutenant and second lieutenant (when combined with the number authorized for general officer grades under section 12004 of this title)	35 percent

Table C.1—Continued

Topic	Statute	Policy
Reserve— full-time control grades 10 U.S.C. 12011(a)(1)	Of the total number of members of a reserve component who are serving on full-time reserve component duty at the end of any fiscal year, the number of those members who may be serving in each of the grades of major, lieutenant colonel, and colonel may not, as of the end of that fiscal year, exceed the number determined in accordance with the following table:	

Table C.1—Continued

Topic	Statute	Policy
Regular—time in grade 10 U.S.C. 619(a)	(1) An officer who is on the active-duty list of the Army, Air Force, or Marine Corps and holds a permanent appointment in the grade of second lieutenant or first lieutenant or is on the active-duty list of the Navy and holds a permanent appointment in the grade of ensign or lieutenant (junior grade) may not be promoted to the next higher permanent grade until he has completed the following period of service in the grade in which he holds a permanent appointment: (A) Eighteen months, in the case of an officer holding a permanent appointment in the grade of second lieutenant or ensign. (B) Two years, in the case of an officer holding a permanent appointment in the grade of first lieutenant or lieutenant (junior grade), except that the minimum period of service in effect under this subparagraph before October 1, 2008, shall be eighteen months. (2) Subject to paragraph (4), an officer who is on the active-duty list of the Army, Air Force, or Marine Corps and holds a permanent appointment in a grade above first lieutenant or is on the active-duty list of the Navy and holds a permanent appointment in a grade above lieutenant (junior grade) may not be considered for selection for promotion to the next higher permanent grade until he has completed the following period of service in the grade in which he holds a permanent appointment: (A) Three years, in the case of an officer of the Army, Air Force, or Marine Corps holding a permanent appointment in the grade of captain, major, or lieutenant colonel or of an officer of the Navy holding a permanent appointment in the grade of lieutenant, lieutenant commander, or commander. . . . (3) When the needs of the service require, the Secretary of the military department concerned may prescribe a longer period of service in grade for eligibility for promotion, in the case of officers to whom paragraph (1) applies, or for eligibility for consideration for promotion, in the case of officers to whom paragraph (2) applies. (4) The Secretary of the military department concerned may waive paragraph (2) to the extent necessary to assure that officers described in subparagraph (A) of such paragraph have at least two opportunities for consideration for promotion to the next higher grade as officers below the promotion zone.	DoDI 1320.13 Promotion opportunities within each grade and competitive category should be relatively similar over the next five years. Promotion timing and opportunity may vary by competitive category, but they should be relatively similar over a period of five years within a competitive category. The desired ADL promotion timing and selection rates for grades of O-6 and below are as follows:

Promotion to	Timing	Time in Grade	Opportunity
O-4	9–11 years	3 years	80%
O-5	15–17 years	3 years	70%
O-6	21–23 years	3 years	50%

Table C.1—Continued

Topic	Statute	Policy
Reserve—time in grade 10 U.S.C. 14303	(a) Officers in Pay Grades O-1 and O-2. An officer who is on the reserve active-status list of the Army, Navy, Air Force, or Marine Corps and holds a permanent appointment in the grade of second lieutenant or first lieutenant as a reserve officer of the Army, Air Force, or Marine Corps, or in the grade of ensign or lieutenant (junior grade) as a reserve officer of the Navy, may not be promoted to the next higher grade, or granted Federal recognition in that grade, until the officer has completed the following years of service in grade: (1) Eighteen months, in the case of an officer holding a permanent appointment in the grade of second lieutenant or ensign. (2) Two years, in the case of an officer holding a permanent appointment in the grade of first lieutenant or lieutenant (junior grade). (b) Officers in Pay Grades O-3 and Above. Subject to subsection (d), an officer who is on the reserve active-status list of the Army, Air Force, or Marine Corps and holds a permanent appointment in a grade above first lieutenant, or who is on the reserve active-status list of the Navy in a grade above lieutenant (junior grade), may not be considered for selection for promotion to the next higher grade, or examined for Federal recognition in the next higher grade, until the officer has completed the following years of service in grade: (1) Three years, in the case of an officer of the Army, Air Force, or Marine Corps holding a permanent appointment in the grade of captain, major, or lieutenant colonel or in the case of a reserve officer of the Navy holding a permanent appointment in the grade of lieutenant, lieutenant commander, or commander. . . . (c) Authority to Lengthen Minimum Period in Grade. The Secretary concerned may prescribe a period of service in grade for eligibility for promotion, in the case of officers to whom subsection (a) applies, or for eligibility for consideration for promotion, in the case of officers to whom subsection (b) applies, that is longer than the applicable period specified in that subsection. (d) Waivers to Ensure Two Below-the-Zone Considerations. Subject to section 14307(b) of this title, the Secretary of the military department concerned may waive subsection (b) to the extent necessary to ensure that officers described in paragraph (1) of that subsection have at least two opportunities for consideration for promotion to the next higher grade as officers below the promotion zone.	

Table C.1—Continued

Topic	Statute	Policy
Regular and Reserve— promotion zones defined 10 U.S.C. 645 10 U.S.C. 14302	(1) The term "promotion zone" means a promotion eligibility category consisting of the officers on an active-duty list in the same grade and competitive category— (A) who— (i) in the case of officers in grades below colonel, for officers of the Army, Air Force, and Marine Corps, or captain, for officers of the Navy, have neither (I) failed of selection for promotion to the next higher grade, nor (II) been removed from a list of officers recommended for promotion to that grade (other than after having been placed on that list after a selection from below the promotion zone); or (ii) in the case of officers in the grade of colonel or brigadier general, for officers of the Army, Air Force, and Marine Corps, or captain or rear admiral (lower half), for officers of the Navy, have neither (I) not been recommended for promotion to the next higher grade when considered in the promotion zone, nor (II) been removed from a list of officers recommended for promotion to that grade (other than after having been placed on that list after a selection from below the promotion zone); and (B) are senior to the officer designated by the Secretary of the military department concerned to be the junior officer in the promotion zone eligible for consideration for promotion to the next higher grade. (2) The term "officers above the promotion zone" means a group of officers on an active-duty list in the same grade and competitive category who— (A) are eligible for consideration for promotion to the next higher grade; (B) are in the same grade as those officers in the promotion zone for that competitive category; and (C) are senior to the senior officer in the promotion zone for that competitive category. (3) The term "officers below the promotion zone" means a group of officers on the active-duty list in the same grade and competitive category who— (A) are eligible for consideration for promotion to the next higher grade; (B) are in the same grade as the officers in the promotion zone for that competitive category; and (C) are junior to the junior officer in the promotion zone for that competitive category. [similar wording for reserve officers]	

Table C.1—Continued

Topic	Statute	Policy
Regular—primary zone 10 U.S.C. 623	(b) The Secretary concerned shall determine the number of officers in the promotion zone for officers serving in any grade and competitive category from among officers who are eligible for promotion in that grade and competitive category. Such determination shall be made on the basis of an estimate of— (1) the number of officers needed in that competitive category in the next higher grade in each of the next five years; (2) the number of officers to be serving in that competitive category in the next higher grade in each of the next five years; (3) in the case of a promotion zone for officers to be promoted to a grade to which section 523 of this title is applicable, the number of officers authorized for such grade under such section to be on active duty on the last day of each of the next five fiscal years; and (4) the number of officers that should be placed in that promotion zone in each of the next five years to provide to officers in those years relatively similar opportunity for promotion.	DoDI 1320.14 Numbers to Be Recommended for Promotion a. Numbers to be Recommended for Promotion. Before establishing the number of officers that may be recommended for promotion to any grade within a competitive category by a promotion selection board convened pursuant to sections 611(a) and 14101(a) of Reference (c), the Secretary of the Military Department concerned, in accordance with sections 622 and 14307(a) of Reference (c), will determine: (1) The number of positions needed to accomplish mission objectives that require officers of the competitive category being considered and in the grade to which the board will recommend officers for promotion. (2) The estimated number of officers needed to fill vacancies in such positions when the selected officers will be promoted. (3) The number of officers authorized by the Secretary of the Military Department concerned to serve on active duty or in an active status in the grade and competitive category under consideration. b. Guidelines. The guidelines set out in paragraphs 3b(1) through 3b(5) of this enclosure will apply to the determinations required in paragraphs 3a(1) through 3a(3) of this enclosure. (1) Requirements for each grade and competitive category are the validated numbers needed based on skill and experience considerations. (2) Estimated vacancies include unfilled requirements at higher grades. (3) The number of officers authorized to serve on active duty or in an active status in a grade and competitive category may be set lower than actual Military Department requirements based on grade limitations established in Reference (c). The number authorized also may be set higher than actual requirements when warranted by promotion flow considerations in a specific competitive category. (4) The officer inventory should reflect the appropriate distribution of officers by grade, experience, and skill. DoDI 1320.14, December 11, 2013 Change 1, March 7, 2018 Enclosure 3 (5) Promotion opportunity and timing, as determined by the Secretary of the Military Department concerned, may vary based on needs. It is desirable

Table C.1—Continued

Topic	Statute	Policy
		that the promotion opportunity and timing of officers serving on the ADL be consistent with the guidelines included in the enclosure of Reference (f)(e). For Reserve Component officers, promotions are based on force requirements. The Secretary of the Military Department concerned will determine the timing and opportunity variables for promotion. c. Annual Promotion Plans. The Military Departments will develop annual promotion plans pursuant to sections 622, 623, 14305, and 14307 of Reference (c) and paragraph 3a of this enclosure.
Reserve—primary zone, mandatory consideration 10 U.S.C. 14305	(b) Number in the Zone. The Secretary concerned shall determine the number of officers in the promotion zone for officers serving in any grade and competitive category from among officers who are eligible for promotion in that grade and competitive category under the provisions of sections 14303 and 14304 of this title and who are otherwise eligible for promotion. (c) Factors in Determining Number in the Zone. The Secretary's determination under subsection (b) shall be made on the basis of an estimate of the following: (1) The number of officers needed in that competitive category in the next higher grade in each of the next five years. (2) In the case of a promotion zone for officers to be promoted to a grade to which the maximum years of in grade criteria established in section 14304 of this title apply, the number of officers in that competitive category who are required to be considered for selection for promotion to the next higher grade under that section. (3) The number of officers that should be placed in the promotion zone in each of the next five years to provide to officers in those years relatively similar opportunities for promotion.	
Reserve—primary zone, running-mate system 10 U.S.C. 14306(b)	An officer to whom a running mate system applies shall be assigned as a running mate an officer of the same grade on the active-duty list of the same armed force. The officer on the reserve active-status list is in the promotion zone and is eligible for consideration for promotion to the next higher grade by a selection board convened under section 14101(a) of this title when that officer's running mate is in or above the promotion zone established for that officer's grade under chapter 36 of this title.	

Table C.1—Continued

Topic	Statute	Policy
Regular—BPZ 10 U.S.C. 616(b)	The Secretary of the military department concerned shall establish the number of officers such a selection board may recommend for promotion from among officers being considered from below the promotion zone in any competitive category. Such number may not exceed the number equal to 10 percent of the maximum number of officers that the board is authorized to recommend for promotion in such competitive category, except that the Secretary of Defense may authorize a greater number, not to exceed 15 percent of the total number of officers that the board is authorized to recommend for promotion, if the Secretary of Defense determines that the needs of the service so require. If the number determined under this subsection is less than one, the board may recommend one such officer. The number of officers recommended for promotion from below the promotion zone does not increase the maximum number of officers which the board is authorized under section 615 of this title to recommend for promotion.	DoDI 1320.14, December 11, 2013 Change 1, March 7, 2018 That the number of officers in any competitive category who have been recommended for promotion and are below the promotion zone may not exceed 10 percent of the maximum number of officers to be recommended for promotion in such competitive category, except as permitted in accordance with this instruction. (2) If the Secretary of the Military Department concerned determines that the needs of the Military Service concerned require additional recommendations from below the promotion zone, he or she may, with the approval of the Secretary of Defense, recommend a greater number. In that case, the number of officers selected may not exceed 15 percent of the total number of the officers that the selection board is authorized to recommend for promotion.
Reserve—BPZ 10 U.S.C. 14307(b)	When selection from below the promotion zone is authorized, the Secretary shall establish the number of officers that may be recommended for promotion from below the promotion zone in each competitive category to be considered. That number may not exceed the number equal to 10 percent of the maximum number of officers that the board is authorized to recommend for promotion in such competitive category, except that the Secretary of Defense may authorize a greater number, not to exceed 15 percent of the total number of officers that the board is authorized to recommend for promotion, if the Secretary of Defense determines that the needs of the armed force concerned so require. If the maximum number determined under this paragraph is less than one, the board may recommend one officer for promotion from below the promotion zone.	

Table C.1—Continued

Topic	Statute	Policy
Reserve—BPZ, running-mate system 10 U.S.C. 14306(c)	If the Secretary of the Navy authorizes the selection of officers for promotion from below the promotion zone in accordance with section 14307 of this title, the number of officers to be considered from below the zone may be established through the application of the running mate system or otherwise as the Secretary determines to be appropriate to meet the needs of the Navy or Marine Corps.	SECNAVINST 1420.1B Navy officers who would be eligible for consideration by a promotion board as an in-zone or above-zone officer with less than one year of placement on the ADL will be deferred unless they specifically request consideration. Navy and Marine Corps precepts specify the maximum number or percentage (as applicable) of officers in each grade and competitive category that could be recommended by their respective promotion boards.

Promotion to	Flow Point	Opportunity
O-4	9–11 years	70–90%
O-5	15–17 years	60–80%
O-6	21–23 years	40–60%

The promotion flow point for the Medical Corps and Dental Corps will normally be six years service in grade based on date of rank.
Years of active commissioned service and entry grade credits count towards flow point. Promotion opportunity may be set temporarily outside above guidelines when necessary to meet or maintain authorized grade strength.
Zones for promotion to O-6 and below for RASL officers shall be established with a running mate system.

Topic	Statute	Policy
Regular— competitive categories 10 U.S.C. 621	Under regulations prescribed by the Secretary of Defense, the Secretary of each military department shall establish competitive categories for promotion. Each officer whose name appears on an active-duty list shall be carried in a competitive category of officers. Officers in the same competitive category shall compete among themselves for promotion.	DoDI 1320.14 Service Secretaries may set the number of officers authorized for each grade of each competitive category lower than actual requirements in order to meet statutory grade limitations, or higher than actual requirements when warranted by promotion flow considerations within a competitive category

Table C.1—Continued

Topic	Statute	Policy
Reserve— competitive categories 10 U.S.C. 144005	Each officer whose name appears on a reserve active-status list shall be placed in a competitive category. The competitive categories for each armed force shall be specified by the Secretary of the military department concerned under regulations prescribed by the Secretary of Defense. Officers in the same competitive category shall compete among themselves for promotion.	
Reserve— position vacancies (mandatory promotion boards) 10 U.S.C. 14308(e)	Army Reserve and Air Force Reserve Promotions to Fill Vacancies. Subject to this section and to section 14311(e) of this title, and under regulations prescribed by the Secretary of the military department concerned— (1) an officer in the Army Reserve or the Air Force Reserve who is on a promotion list as a result of selection for promotion by a mandatory promotion board convened under section 14101(a) of this title or a board convened under section 14502 or chapter 36 of this title may be promoted at any time to fill a vacancy in a position to which the officer is assigned; and (2) an officer in a grade below colonel in the Army Reserve or the Air Force Reserve who is on a promotion list as a result of selection for promotion by a vacancy promotion board convened under section 14101(a) of this title may be promoted at any time to fill the vacancy for which the officer was selected.	DoDI 1320.14 (3) Voluntary delay of promotion in accordance with section 14312 of Reference (c) and involuntary delay of promotion in accordance with section 14311 of Reference (c) for these reasons: (a) Strength limitations pursuant to section 14311(e)(1) of Reference (c). (b) The duty assignment authorized grade is lower than the grade to which the officer is selected for promotion pursuant to section 14311(e)(2) of Reference (c). In such situations, the Secretary of the Military Department concerned may approve an over-grade waiver for the officer subject to the limitations in section 12011 of Reference (c). (c) Position vacancy promotion, as described in sections 14101(a)(2) and 14315 of Reference (c). (d) Federal recognition pertaining to the Army National Guard of the United States and the Air National Guard of the United States, as covered in section 14316 of Reference (c). (e) Running mate system of the Navy Reserve and Marine Corps Reserve, as covered in section 14306 of Reference (c).

Table C.1—Continued

Topic	Statute	Policy
Reserve—position vacancy promotion boards 10 U.S.C. 14315	(a) Officers Eligible for Consideration for Vacancy Promotions Below Brigadier General. A reserve officer of the Army who is in the Army Reserve, or a reserve officer of the Air Force who is in the Air Force Reserve, who is on the reserve active-status list in the grade of first lieutenant, captain, major, or lieutenant colonel is eligible for consideration for promotion to the next higher grade under this section if each of the following applies: (1) The officer is occupying or, under regulations prescribed by the Secretary concerned, has been recommended to occupy a position in the same competitive category as the officer and for which a grade higher than the one held by that officer is authorized. (2) The officer is fully qualified to meet all requirements for the position as established by the Secretary of the military department concerned. (3) The officer has held the officer's present grade for the minimum period of service prescribed in section 14303 of this title for eligibility for consideration for promotion to the higher grade. . . . (d) Effect of Nonselection. An officer who is considered for promotion under this section and is not selected shall not be considered to have failed of selection for promotion.	

Table C.2
Tenure-Related Statutory and Policy Provisions by Topic

Topic	Statute	Policy
Regular—up or out 10 U.S.C. 632(a)	Except an officer of the Navy and Marine Corps who is an officer designated for limited duty (to whom section 5596(e) or 6383 of this title applies) and except as provided under section 637(a) of this title, each officer of the Army, Air Force, or Marine Corps on the active-duty list who holds the grade of captain or major, and each officer of the Navy on the active-duty list who holds the grade of lieutenant or lieutenant commander, who has failed of selection for promotion to the next higher grade for the second time and whose name is not on a list of officers recommended for promotion to the next higher grade shall— (1) except as provided in paragraph (3) and in subsection (c), be discharged on the date requested by him and approved by the Secretary concerned, which date shall be not later than the first day of the seventh calendar month beginning after the month in which the President approves the report of the board which considered him for the second time; (2) if he is eligible for retirement under any provision of law, be retired under that law on the date requested by him and approved by the Secretary concerned, which date shall be not later than the first day of the seventh calendar month beginning after the month in which the President approves the report of the board which considered him for the second time; or (3) if on the date on which he is to be discharged under paragraph (1) he is within two years of qualifying for retirement under section 3911, 6323, or 8911 of this title, be retained on active duty until he is qualified for retirement and then retired under that section, unless he is sooner retired or discharged under another provision of law.	DoDI 1320.10: Officers who are unqualified for promotion to the grade of O-2 are to be discharged. However, such officers are to be retained on the active-duty list (ADL) or reserve active-status list (RASL) for a minimum of 6 months from the date the promotion would have occurred. The officer must be discharged at the end of 18 months from the date the promotion would have occurred unless found qualified for promotion. DoDI 1332.30 It is DOD policy to separate from service officers in the Regular and Reserve Components of the military who are unable to meet standards of duty, performance, and integrity. Service Secretaries may discharge officers on the ADL or RASL with less than 6 years of commissioned service when there is a need to reduce the number of officers to meet force size requirements. A commissioned officer may be involuntarily separated if found to be substandard in the following ways: performance of duty, efficiency, leadership, response to training, attitude or character, maintenance of satisfactory progress while in a skills-awarding program, or acts of professional or moral misconduct. A commissioned officer may also be involuntarily separated if retention of that officer is found to be inconsistent with national security interests.

Table C.2—Continued

Topic	Statute	Policy
Reserve—up or out, O-3 10 U.S.C. 14505	Unless retained as provided in section 12646 or 12686 of this title, a captain on the reserve active-status list of the Army, Air Force, or Marine Corps or a lieutenant on the reserve active-status list of the Navy who has failed of selection for promotion to the next higher grade for the second time and whose name is not on a list of officers recommended for promotion to the next higher grade and who has not been selected for continuation on the reserve active-status list under section 14701 of this title, shall be separated in accordance with section 14513 of this title not later than the first day of the seventh month after the month in which the President approves the report of the board which considered the officer for the second time.	
Regular—selective continuation 10 U.S.C. 637(a)	(1) An officer subject to discharge or retirement in accordance with section 632 of this title may, subject to the needs of the service, be continued on active duty if he is selected for continuation on active duty by a selection board convened under section 611(b) of this title. (2) An officer who holds the regular grade of captain in the Army, Air Force, or Marine Corps, or the regular grade of lieutenant in the Navy, and who is subject to discharge or retirement in accordance with section 632 of this title may not be continued on active duty under this subsection for a period which extends beyond the last day of the month in which he completes 20 years of active commissioned service unless he is promoted to the regular grade of major or lieutenant commander, respectively. (3) An officer who holds the regular grade of major or lieutenant commander who is subject to discharge or retirement in accordance with section 632 of this title may not be continued on active duty under this subsection for a period which extends beyond the last day of the month in which he completes 24 years of active commissioned service unless he is promoted to the regular grade of lieutenant colonel or commander, respectively.	DoDI 1320.08: The minimum periods of continuation of officers are as follows:

Officer Grade	Officers on ADL
O-3	2 yrs unless within 2 yrs of qualifying for retirement, in which case it can be less. Officers cannot exceed 20 yrs ACS.
O-4	Long enough to qualify for retirement if within 6 yrs. Officers cannot exceed 24 yrs ACS.
O-5 to O-6	2 yrs unless within 2 yrs of qualifying for retirement, in which case it can be less.
O-7 to O-10	Based on needs of the military service.

Table C.2—Continued

Topic	Statute	Policy
Reserve—selective continuation 10 U.S.C. 14701(a)	(1)(A) A reserve officer of the Army, Navy, Air Force, or Marine Corps described in subparagraph (B) who is required to be removed from the reserve active-status list under section 14504 of this title, or a reserve officer of the Army, Navy, Air Force, or Marine Corps who is required to be removed from the reserve active-status list under section 14505, 14506, or 14507 of this title, may be considered for continuation on the reserve active-status list under regulations prescribed by the Secretary of Defense. . . . (2) A reserve officer who holds the grade of captain in the Army, Air Force, or Marine Corps or the grade of lieutenant in the Navy and who is subject to separation under section 14513 of this title may not be continued on the reserve active-status list under this subsection for a period which extends beyond the last day of the month in which the officer completes 20 years of commissioned service. (3) A reserve officer who holds the grade of major or lieutenant commander and who is subject to separation under section 14513 of this title may not be continued on the reserve active-status list under this subsection for a period which extends beyond the last day of the month in which the officer completes 24 years of commissioned service. (4) A reserve officer who holds the grade of lieutenant colonel or commander and who is subject to separation under section 14514 of this title may not be continued on the reserve active-status list under this subsection for a period which extends beyond the last day of the month in which the officer completes 33 years of commissioned service. (5) A reserve officer who holds the grade of colonel in the Army, Air Force, or Marine Corps or the grade of captain in the Navy and who is subject to separation under section 14514 of this title may not be continued on the reserve active-status list under this subsection for a period which extends beyond the last day of the month in which the officer completes 35 years of commissioned service.	DoDI 1320.08 The minimum periods of continuation of officers are as follows:

Officer Grade	Officers on RASL
O-3	Subject to the needs of the military serviceOfficers on RASL.
O-4	Subject to the needs of the military serviceOfficers cannot exceed 20 YCS [years of commissioned service]. Officers cannot exceed 24 YCS.
O-5	Subject to the needs of the military serviceOfficers cannot exceed 24 YCS. Officers cannot exceed 33 YCS.
O-6	Subject to the needs of the military service Officers cannot exceed 35 YCS.
O-7 to O-10	Subject to the needs of the military service.

Service Secretaries can retain reserve officers who serve in medical, dental, veterinary, chaplain, and nursing or biomedical capacities up until the officers turn 68 years of age.

Table C.2—Continued

Topic	Statute	Policy
Regular—SERB eligibility 10 U.S.C. 638(a)	(1) A regular officer on the active-duty list of the Army, Navy, Air Force, or Marine Corps may be considered for selective early retirement by a selection board convened under section 611(b) of this title if the officer is described in any of subparagraphs (A) through (D) as follows: (A) An officer holding the regular grade of lieutenant colonel or commander who has failed of selection for promotion to the grade of colonel or, in the case of an officer of the Navy, captain two or more times and whose name is not on a list of officers recommended for promotion. (B) An officer holding the regular grade of colonel or, in the case of an officer of the Navy, captain who has served at least four years of active duty in that grade and whose name is not on a list of officers recommended for promotion.	DoDI 1332.32 Service Secretaries may convene boards to select Regular or Reserve officers for early retirement or removal from active status. For the Army and Air National Guards, the constitutional prerogatives of the States shall be taken into consideration for decisions about selective early retirement or separation from active status.
Regular—SERB numbers 10 U.S.C. 638(a)(2)	The Secretary of the military department concerned shall specify the number of officers described in paragraphs (1)(A) and (1)(B) which a selection board convened under section 611(b) of this title may recommend for early retirement. Such number may not be more than 30 percent of the number of officers considered in each grade in each competitive category.	
Regular—SERB considerations 10 U.S.C. 638(c)	So long as an officer in a grade below brigadier general or rear admiral (lower half) holds the same grade, he may not be considered for early retirement under this section more than once in any five-year period.	Marine Corps: MCO P1900.16F, MARCORSEPMAN (1) Officers may be excluded from consideration if they have an approved request for voluntary retirement, or are subject to mandatory retirement during the fiscal year in which the selective early retirement board is convened or during the following fiscal year. (2) No more than 30 percent of the officers considered in each grade, in each competitive category may be selected. (3) Officers selected will be retired no later than the first day of the seventh month following the month in which the Secretary of the Navy approves the report of the board. (4) Only officers who have twice failed of selection to the next higher grade will be considered eligible.

Table C.2—Continued

Topic	Statute	Policy
Regular—SERB zone 10 U.S.C. 638(e) (2)(A)	Such regulations shall require that when the Secretary of the military department concerned submits a list of officers to a selection board convened under section 611(b) of this title to consider officers for selection for early retirement under this section, such list (except as provided in subparagraph (B)) shall include each officer on the active-duty list in the same grade and competitive category whose position on the active-duty list is between that of the most junior officer in that grade and competitive category whose name is submitted to the board and that of the most senior officer in that grade and competitive category whose name is submitted to the board.	Army: AR 600-8-24 Army officers may be considered for selective early retirement by a duly convened board under the following conditions: O-3 officers not currently recommended for promotion who are retirement-eligible or will be within 2 years of active Federal service. O-4 officers not currently recommended for promotion who are retirement-eligible or will be within 2 years of active Federal service. O-5 officers who have been twice non-selected for promotion and are not currently recommended for promotion O-6 officers with at least 4 years of service in that grade and are not currently recommended for promotion O-7 officers with at least 3.5 years of service in that grade and are not currently recommended for promotion O-8 officers with at least 3.5 years of service Navy: SECNAVINST 1420.1B SECNAV [Secretary of the Navy] convenes selection boards to recommend officers for selective early retirement or separation based on recommendations from the CNO [Chief of Naval Operations] and CMC [Commandant of the Marine Corps]. Officers on the ADL in grades O-5 to O-8 or on the RASL in grades O-7 to O-8 may be considered for involuntary early retirement. Officers on the RASL in any grade may be considered for involuntary separation. RASL officers who are recommended for involuntary separation shall be discharged if unqualified for transfer to the Retired Reserve.

Table C.2—Continued

Topic	Statute	Policy
Regular—force shaping 10 U.S.C. 647	(a) Authority. The Secretary concerned may, solely for the purpose of restructuring an armed force under the jurisdiction of that Secretary— (1) discharge an officer described in subsection (b); or (2) transfer such an officer from the active-duty list of that armed force to the reserve active-status list of a reserve component of that armed force. (b) Covered Officers. (1) The authority under this section may be exercised in the case of an officer who— (A) has completed not more than six years of service as a commissioned officer in the armed forces; or (B) has completed more than six years of service as a commissioned officer in the armed forces, but has not completed a minimum service obligation applicable to that member. (2) In this subsection, the term "minimum service obligation" means the initial period of required active duty service together with any additional period of required active duty service incurred during the initial period of required active duty service.	
Regular— enhanced authority 10 U.S.C. 638a	(b) Actions which the Secretary of a military department may take with respect to officers of an armed force when authorized to do so under subsection (a) are the following: (1) Shortening the period of the continuation on active duty established under section 637 of this title for a regular officer who is serving on active duty pursuant to a selection under that section for continuation on active duty. (2) Providing that regular officers on the active-duty list may be considered for early retirement by a selection board convened under section 611(b) of this title in the case of officers described in any of subparagraphs (A) through (C) as follows: (A) Officers in the regular grade of lieutenant colonel or commander who have failed of selection for promotion at least one time and whose names are not on a list of officers recommended for promotion. (B) Officers in the regular grade of colonel or, in the case of the Navy, captain who have served on active duty in that grade for at least two years and whose names are not on a list of officers recommended for promotion.	

Table C.2—Continued

Topic	Statute	Policy
	(C) Officers, other than those described in subparagraphs (A) and (B), holding a regular grade below the grade of colonel, or in the case of the Navy, captain, who are eligible for retirement under section 3911, 6323, or 8911 of this title, or who after two additional years or less of active service would be eligible for retirement under one of those sections and whose names are not on a list of officers recommended for promotion.	

(3) Convening selection boards under section 611(b) of this title to consider for discharge regular officers on the active-duty list in a grade below lieutenant colonel or commander—

(A) who have served at least one year of active duty in the grade currently held;

(B) whose names are not on a list of officers recommended for promotion; and

(C) who are not eligible to be retired under any provision of law (other than by reason of eligibility pursuant to section 4403 of the National Defense Authorization Act for Fiscal Year 1993) and are not within two years of becoming so eligible.

(4) Convening selection boards under section 611(b) of this title to consider for early retirement or discharge regular officers on the active-duty list in a grade below lieutenant colonel or commander—

(A) who have served at least one year of active duty in the grade currently held; and

(B) whose names are not on a list of officers recommended for promotion.

(c)

(1) In the case of an action under subsection (b)(2), the total number of officers described in that subsection that a selection board convened under section 611(b) of this title pursuant to the authority of that subsection may recommend for early retirement may not be more than 30 percent of the number of officers considered in each grade in each competitive category. . . .

(3) In the case of an action under subsection (b)(2), the Secretary of the military department concerned may submit to a selection board convened pursuant to that subsection—

(A) the names of all eligible officers described in that subsection in a particular grade and competitive category; or

(B) the names of all eligible officers described in that subsection in a particular grade and competitive category who

Table C.2—Continued

Topic	Statute	Policy
	are also in particular year groups, specialties, or retirement categories, or any combination thereof, within that competitive category.	

(4) In the case of an action under subsection (b)(2), the Secretary of Defense may also authorize the Secretary of the military department concerned to waive the five-year period specified in section 638(c) of this title if the Secretary of Defense determines that it is necessary for the Secretary of that military department to have such authority in order to meet mission needs.

(d)

(1) In the case of an action under subsection (b)(3), the Secretary of the military department concerned may submit to a selection board convened pursuant to that subsection—

(A) the names of all officers described in that subsection in a particular grade and competitive category; or

(B) the names of all officers described in that subsection in a particular grade and competitive category who also are in particular year groups or specialties, or both, within that competitive category.

(2) The total number of officers to be recommended for discharge by a selection board convened pursuant to subsection (b)(3) may not be more than 30 percent of the number of officers considered.

(3) An officer who is recommended for discharge by a selection board convened pursuant to the authority of subsection (b)(3) and whose discharge is approved by the Secretary concerned shall be discharged on a date specified by the Secretary concerned.

(4) Selection of officers for discharge under this subsection shall be based on the needs of the service.

(e)

(1) In the case of action under subsection (b)(4), the Secretary of the military department concerned shall specify the total number of officers described in that subsection that a selection board convened under section 611(b) of this title pursuant to the authority of that subsection may recommend for early retirement or discharge. Officers who are eligible, or are within two years of becoming eligible, to be retired under any provision of law (other than by reason of eligibility pursuant to section 4403 of the National Defense Authorization Act for Fiscal Year 1993 (Public Law 102-484)), if selected by

Table C.2—Continued

Topic	Statute	Policy
	the board, shall be retired or retained until becoming eligible to retire under section 3911, 6323, or 8911 of this title, and those officers who are otherwise ineligible to retire under any provision of law shall, if selected by the board, be discharged. (2) In the case of action under subsection (b)(4), the Secretary of the military department concerned may submit to a selection board convened pursuant to that subsection— (A) the names of all eligible officers described in that subsection, whether or not they are eligible to be retired under any provision of law, in a particular grade and competitive category; or (B) the names of all eligible officers described in that subsection in a particular grade and competitive category, whether or not they are eligible to be retired under any provision of law, who are also in particular year groups, specialties, or retirement categories, or any combination thereof, with that competitive category. (3) The number of officers specified under paragraph (1) may not be more than 30 percent of the number of officers considered.	

Table C.2—Continued

Topic	Statute	Policy

Reserve—SERB 10 U.S.C. 14704	(a) Boards to Recommend for Removal from Active-Status List
	(1) Whenever the Secretary of the military department concerned determines that there are in any reserve component under the jurisdiction of the Secretary too many officers in any grade and competitive category who have at least 30 years of service computed under section 14706 of this title or at least 20 years of service computed under section 12732 of this title, the Secretary may convene a selection board under section 14101(b) of this title to consider officers on the reserve active-status list who are in that grade and competitive category, and who have that amount of service, for the purpose of recommending officers by name for removal from that list.
	(2) Except as provided in paragraph (3), the list of officers in a reserve component whose names are submitted to a board under paragraph (1) shall include each officer on the reserve active-status list for that reserve component in the same grade and competitive category whose position on the reserve active-status list is between—
	    (A) that of the most junior officer in that grade and competitive category whose name is submitted to the board; and
	    (B) that of the most senior officer in that grade and competitive category whose name is submitted to the board. . . .
	(b) Specification of Number of Officers Who May Be Recommended for Separation. The Secretary of the military department concerned shall specify the number of officers described in subsection (a)(1) that a board may recommend for separation under subsection (c).	

Reserve—enhanced authority 10 U.S.C. 638a(c)(2)	In the case of an action authorized under subsection (b)(2), the Secretary of Defense may also authorize the Secretary of the military department concerned when convening a selection board under section 611(b) of this title to consider regular officers on the active-duty list for early retirement to include within the officers to be considered by the board reserve officers on the active-duty list on the same basis as regular officers.	

Table C.2—Continued

Topic	Statute	Policy
Regular— retirement for age 10 U.S.C. 1251	Unless retired or separated earlier, each regular commissioned officer of the Army, Navy, Air Force, or Marine Corps (other than an officer covered by section 1252 of this title or a commissioned warrant officer) serving in a grade below brigadier general or rear admiral (lower half), in the case of an officer in the Navy, shall be retired on the first day of the month following the month in which the officer becomes 62 years of age.	
Reserve— separation for age 10 U.S.C. 14509	Each reserve officer of the Army, Navy, Air Force, or Marine Corps in a grade below brigadier general or rear admiral (lower half) who has not been recommended for promotion to the grade of brigadier general or rear admiral (lower half) and is not a member of the Retired Reserve shall, on the last day of the month in which that officer becomes 62 years of age, be separated in accordance with section 14515 of this title.	
Regular— retirement for years of service, O-5 10 U.S.C. 633	(a) Except as provided in subsection (b) and as provided under section 637(b) or 637a of this title, each officer of the Regular Army, Regular Air Force, or Regular Marine Corps who holds the regular grade of lieutenant colonel, and each officer of the Regular Navy who holds the regular grade of commander, who is not on a list of officers recommended for promotion to the regular grade of colonel or captain, respectively, shall, if not earlier retired, be retired on the first day of the month after the month in which he completes 28 years of active commissioned service. (b) Exceptions.—Subsection (a) does not apply to the following: (1) An officer of the Navy or Marine Corps who is an officer designated for limited duty to whom section 5596(e) or 6383 of this title applies. (2) An officer of the Navy or Marine Corps who is a permanent professor at the United States Naval Academy.	

Table C.2—Continued

Topic	Statute	Policy
Regular— retirement for years of service, O-6 10 U.S.C. 634	(a) Except as provided in subsection (b) and as provided under section 637(b) or 637a of this title, each officer of the Regular Army, Regular Air Force, or Regular Marine Corps who holds the regular grade of colonel, and each officer of the Regular Navy who holds the regular grade of captain, who is not on a list of officers recommended for promotion to the regular grade of brigadier general or rear admiral (lower half), respectively, shall, if not earlier retired, be retired on the first day of the month after the month in which he completes 30 years of active commissioned service. (b) Exceptions. Subsection (a) does not apply to the following: (1) An officer of the Navy who is designated for limited duty to whom section 6383(a)(4) of this title applies. (2) An officer of the Navy or Marine Corps who is a permanent professor at the United States Naval Academy.	
Regular— continuation to 40 years of service 10 U.S.C. 637a	(a) In General. The Secretary of the military department concerned may authorize an officer in a grade above grade O–4 to remain on active duty after the date otherwise provided for the retirement of the officer in section 633, 634, 635, or 636 of this title, as applicable, if the officer has a military occupational specialty, rating, or specialty code in a military specialty designated pursuant to subsection (b). (b) Military Specialties. Each Secretary of a military department shall designate the military specialties in which a military occupational specialty, rating, or specialty code, as applicable, assigned to members of the armed forces under the jurisdiction of such Secretary authorizes the members to be eligible for continuation on active duty as provided in subsection (a). (c) Duration of Continuation. An officer continued on active duty pursuant to this section shall, if not earlier retired, be retired on the first day of the month after the month in which the officer completes 40 years of active service.	

Table C.2—Continued

Topic	Statute	Policy
Reserve— retirement for years of service, O-4 10 U.S.C. 14506	Unless retained as provided in section 12646, 12686, 14701, or 14702 of this title, each reserve officer of the Army, Navy, Air Force, or Marine Corps who holds the grade of major or lieutenant commander who has failed of selection to the next higher grade for the second time and whose name is not on a list of officers recommended for promotion to the next higher grade shall, if not earlier removed from the reserve active-status list, be removed from that list in accordance with section 14513 of this title on the later of (1) the first day of the month after the month in which the officer completes 20 years of commissioned service, or (2) the first day of the seventh month after the month in which the President approves the report of the board which considered the officer for the second time.	
Reserve— retirement for years of service, O-5 or O-6 10 U.S.C. 14507	(a) Lieutenant Colonels and Commanders. Unless continued on the reserve active-status list under section 14701 or 14702 of this title or retained as provided in section 12646 or 12686 of this title, each reserve officer of the Army, Navy, Air Force, or Marine Corps who holds the grade of lieutenant colonel or commander and who is not on a list of officers recommended for promotion to the next higher grade shall (if not earlier removed from the reserve active-status list) be removed from that list under section 14514 of this title on the first day of the month after the month in which the officer completes 28 years of commissioned service. (b) Colonels and Navy Captains. Unless continued on the reserve active-status list under section 14701 or 14702 of this title or retained as provided in section 12646 or 12686 of this title, each reserve officer of the Army, Air Force, or Marine Corps who holds the grade of colonel, and each reserve officer of the Navy who holds the grade of captain, and who is not on a list of officers recommended for promotion to the next higher grade shall (if not earlier removed from the reserve active-status list) be removed from that list under section 14514 of this title on the first day of the month after the month in which the officer completes 30 years of commissioned service. This subsection does not apply to the adjutant general or assistant adjutants general of a State.	

Table C.2—Continued

Topic	Statute	Policy

Career Intermission Pilot Program (CIPP), 2009 NDAA (Pub. L. 110-417, October 14, 2008), Section 533	Pilot Programs on Career Flexibility to Enhance Retention of Members of the Armed Forces.
	
	(a) Pilot Programs Authorized.—
	    (1) In general.—Each Secretary of a military department may carry out pilot programs under which officers and enlisted members of the regular components of the Armed Forces under the jurisdiction of such Secretary may be inactivated from active duty in order to meet personal or professional needs and returned to active duty at the end of such period of inactivation from active duty.
	    (2) Purpose.—The purpose of the pilot programs under this section shall be to evaluate whether permitting inactivation from active duty and greater flexibility in career paths members of the Armed Forces will provide an effective means to enhance retention of members of the Armed Forces and the capacity of the Department of Defense to respond to the personal and professional needs of individual members of the Armed Forces.
	(b) Limitation on Eligible Members.—A member of the Armed Forces is not eligible to participate in a pilot program under this section during any period of service required of the member—
	    (1) under an agreement upon entry of the member on active duty; or
	    (2) due to receipt by the member of a retention bonus as a member qualified in a critical military skill or assigned to a high priority unit under section 355 of title 37, United States Code.
	(c) Limitation on Number of Participants.—Not more than 20 officers and 20 enlisted members of each Armed Force may be selected during each of calendar years 2009 through 2012 to participate in the pilot programs under this section.
	(d) Period of Inactivation From Active Duty; Effect of Inactivation.—
	    (1) Limitation.—The period of inactivation from active duty under a pilot program under this section of a member participating in the pilot program shall be such period as the Secretary of the military department concerned shall specify in the agreement of the member under subsection (e), except that such period may not exceed three years.
	    (2) Exclusion from computation of reserve officer's total years of service.—Any service by a Reserve officer while	

Table C.2—Continued

Topic	Statute	Policy
	participating in a pilot program under this section shall be excluded from computation of the officer's total years of service pursuant to section 4706(a) of title 10, United States Code.	

participating in a pilot program under this section shall be excluded from computation of the officer's total years of service pursuant to section 4706(a) of title 10, United States Code.

(3) Retirement and related purposes.— Any period of participation of a member in a pilot program under this section shall not count toward—

(A) eligibility for retirement or transfer to the Ready Reserve under either chapter 571 or 1223 of title 10, United States Code; or

(B) computation of retired or retainer pay under chapter 71 or 1223 of title 10, United States Code.

(e) Agreement.—Each member of the Armed Forces who participates in a pilot program under this section shall enter into a written agreement with the Secretary of the military department concerned under which agreement that member shall agree as follows:

(1) To accept an appointment or enlist, as applicable, and serve in the Ready Reserve of the Armed Force concerned during the period of the member's inactivation from active duty under the pilot program.

(2) To undergo during the period of the inactivation of the member from active duty under the pilot program such inactive duty training as the Secretary concerned shall require in order to ensure that the member retains proficiency, at a level determined by the Secretary concerned to be sufficient, in the member's military skills, professional qualifications, and physical readiness during the inactivation of the member from active duty.

(3) Following completion of the period of the inactivation of the member from active duty under the pilot program, to serve two months as a member of the Armed Forces on active duty for each month of the period of the inactivation of the member from active duty under the pilot program.

(f) Conditions of Release.— The Secretary of Defense shall issue regulations specifying the guidelines regarding the conditions of release that must be considered and addressed in the agreement required by subsection (e). At a minimum, the Secretary shall prescribe the procedures and standards to be used to instruct a member on the obligations to be assumed by the member under

Table C.2—Continued

Topic	Statute	Policy

paragraph (2) of such subsection while the member is released from active duty.

(g) Order to Active Duty.—Under regulations prescribed by the Secretary of the military department concerned, a member of the Armed Forces participating in a pilot program under this section may, in the discretion of such Secretary, be required to terminate participation in the pilot program and be ordered to active duty.

(h) Pay and Allowances.—

(1) Basic pay.—During each month of participation in a pilot program under this section, a member who participates in the pilot program shall be paid basic pay in an amount equal to two-thirtieths of the amount of monthly basic pay to which the member would otherwise be entitled under section 204 of title 37, United States Code, as a member of the uniformed services on active duty in the grade and years of service of the member when the member commences participation in the pilot program.

(2) Prohibition on receipt of special and incentive pays.—

(A) Prohibition on receipt during participation.—A member who participates in a pilot program shall not, while participating in the pilot program, be paid any special or incentive pay or bonus to which the member is otherwise entitled under an agreement under chapter 5 of title 37, United States Code, that is in force when the member commences participation in the pilot program.

(B) Treatment of required service.—The inactivation from active duty of a member participating in a pilot program shall not be treated as a failure of the member to perform any period of service required of the member in connection with an agreement for a special or incentive pay or bonus under chapter 5 of title 37, United States Code, that is in force when the member commences participation in the pilot program.

(3) Revival of special pays upon return to active duty.—

(A) Revival required.—Subject to subparagraph (B), upon the return of a member to active duty after completion by the member of participation in a pilot program—

(i) any agreement entered into by the member under chapter 5 of title 37, United States Code, for the payment of a

Table C.2—Continued

Topic	Statute	Policy
	special or incentive pay or bonus that was in force when the member commenced participation in the pilot program shall be revived, with the term of such agreement after revival being the period of the agreement remaining to run when the member commenced participation in the pilot program; and	

special or incentive pay or bonus that was in force when the member commenced participation in the pilot program shall be revived, with the term of such agreement after revival being the period of the agreement remaining to run when the member commenced participation in the pilot program; and

(ii) any special or incentive pay or bonus shall be payable to the member in accordance with the terms of the agreement concerned for the term specified in clause (i).

(B) Limitations.—

(i) Limitation at time of return to active duty.—Subparagraph (A) shall not apply to any special or incentive pay or bonus otherwise covered by that subparagraph with respect to a member if, at the time of the return of the member to active duty as described in that subparagraph—

(I) such pay or bonus is no longer authorized by law; or

(II) the member does not satisfy eligibility criteria for such pay or bonus as in effect at the time of the return of the member to active duty.

(ii) Cessation during later service.— Subparagraph (A) shall cease to apply to any special or incentive pay or bonus otherwise covered by that subparagraph with respect to a member if, during the term of the revived agreement of the member under subparagraph (A)(i), such pay or bonus ceases being authorized by law.

(C) Repayment.—A member who is ineligible for payment of a special or incentive pay or bonus covered by this paragraph by reason of subparagraph (B) (i)(II) shall be subject to the requirements for repayment of such pay or bonus in accordance with the terms of the applicable agreement of the member under chapter 5 of title 37, United States Code.

(D) Construction of required service.— Any service required of a member under an agreement covered by this paragraph after the member returns to active duty as described in subparagraph (A) shall be in addition to any service required of the member under an agreement under subsection (e).

(4) Certain travel and transportation allowances.—

(A) In general.—Subject to subparagraph (B), a member who

Table C.2—Continued

Topic	Statute	Policy
	participates in a pilot program is entitled, while participating in the pilot program, to the travel and transportation allowances authorized by section 404 of title 37, United States Code, for—	

participates in a pilot program is entitled, while participating in the pilot program, to the travel and transportation allowances authorized by section 404 of title 37, United States Code, for—

(i) travel performed from the member's residence, at the time of release from active duty to participate in the pilot program, to the location in the United States designated by the member as his residence during the period of participation in the pilot program; and

(ii) travel performed to the member's residence upon return to active duty at the end of the member's participation in the pilot program.

(B) Limitation.—An allowance is payable under this paragraph only with respect to travel of a member to from a single residence.

(i) Promotion.—

(1) Officers.—

(A) Limitation on promotion.—An officer participating in a pilot program under this section shall not, while participating in the pilot program, be eligible for consideration for promotion under chapter 36 or 1405 of title 10, United States Code.

(B) Promotion and rank upon return to active duty.—Upon the return of an officer to active duty after completion by the officer of participation in a pilot program—

(i) the Secretary of the military department concerned shall adjust the officer's date of rank in such manner as the Secretary of Defense shall prescribe in regulations for purposes of this section; and

(ii) the officer shall be eligible for consideration for promotion when officers of the same competitive category, grade, and seniority are eligible for consideration for promotion.

(2) Enlisted members.—An enlisted member participating in a pilot program shall not be eligible for consideration for promotion during the period that—

(A) begins on the date of the member's inactivation from active duty under the pilot program; and

(B) ends at such time after the return of the member to active duty under the pilot program that the member is treatable as eligible for promotion by reason of time in grade and such other requirements as the Secretary of the military department concerned shall prescribe in regulations for purposes of the pilot program.

Table C.2—Continued

Topic	Statute	Policy
	(j) Medical and Dental Care.—A member participating in a pilot program under this section shall, while participating in the pilot program, be treated as a member of the Armed Forces on active duty for a period of more than 30 days for purposes of the entitlement of the member and the member's dependents to medical and dental care under the provisions of chapter 55 of title 10, United States Code.	

Bibliography

Army Regulation 600-8-24, *Officer Transfers and Discharges*, Washington, D.C.: Department of the Army, September 13, 2011. As of January 18, 2019:
https://armypubs.army.mil/epubs/DR_pubs/DR_a/pdf/web/r600_8_24.pdf.

Barno, David, and Nora Bensahel, "Can the U.S. Military Halt Its Brain Drain?" *The Atlantic*, November 5, 2015. As of June 21, 2018:
https://www.theatlantic.com/politics/archive/2015/11/us-military-tries-halt-brain-drain/413965/

Carson, Christopher M., *I Hear What You Are Saying: Analysis of USAF Rated Officer Comments from the 2015 Military Career Decisions Survey*, Santa Monica, Calif.: RAND Corporation, RGSD-397, 2017. As of July 9, 2018:
https://www.rand.org/pubs/rgs_dissertations/RGSD397.html

Department of the Army, *Commissioned Officer Professional Development and Career Management*, Washington, D.C.: Department of the Army, Pamphlet 600-3, December 3, 2014. As of June 27, 2018:
https://www.army.mil/e2/c/downloads/376665.pdf

Department of Defense Instruction 1310.01, *Rank and Seniority of Commissioned Officers*, Washington, D.C.: Department of Defense, July 7, 2017. As of January 18, 2019:
https://www.esd.whs.mil/Portals/54/Documents/DD/issuances/dodi/131001p.pdf

Department of Defense Instruction 1320.08, *Continuation of Commissioned Officers on Active Duty on the Reserve Active-Status List*, Change 1, Washington, D.C.: Department of Defense, October 23, 2018. As of January 18, 2019:
https://www.esd.whs.mil/Portals/54/Documents/DD/issuances/dodi/132008p.pdf?ver=2018-10-23-093853-417

Department of Defense Instruction 1320.10, *Policy on Graduate Education for Military Officers*, Washington, D.C.: Department of Defense, April 29, 2008. As of January 18, 2019:
https://www.esd.whs.mil/Portals/54/Documents/DD/issuances/dodi/132210p.pdf

Department of Defense Instruction 1320.13, *Commissioned Officer Promotion Reports (CORPS)*, Washington, D.C.: Department of Defense, October 30, 2014. As of January 18, 2019:
https://www.esd.whs.mil/Portals/54/Documents/DD/issuances/dodi/132013p.pdf

Department of Defense Instruction 1320.14, Change 1, *Commissioned Officer Promotion Program Procedures*, Washington, D.C.: Department of Defense, March 7, 2018. As of August 22, 2018:
http://www.esd.whs.mil/Directives/issuances/dodi/

Department of Defense Instruction 1322.10, *Policy on Graduate Education for Military Officers*, Washington, D.C.: Department of Defense, April 29, 2008. As of November 29, 2018:
https://www.career-satisfaction.army.mil/resources/pdfs/DoD%20Directive%201322.10_Policy_on _Graduate_Education_For_Military_Officers.pdf

Department of Defense Instruction 1332.30, *Commissioned Officer Administrative Separations*, Washington, D.C.: Department of Defense, May 11, 2018. As of January 18, 2019:
https://www.esd.whs.mil/Portals/54/Documents/DD/issuances/dodi/133230p.pdf?ver=2018-05-11 -101352-010

Department of Defense Instruction 1332.32, *Selective Early Retirement Or Removal of Officers on the Active Duty List, the Warrant Officer Active Duty List, Or the Reserve Active Status List*, Washington, D.C.: Department of Defense, May 12, 2014. As of January 18, 2019:
https://www.esd.whs.mil/Portals/54/Documents/DD/issuances/dodi/133232p.pdf

Department of Defense Instruction 1332.45, *Retention Determinations for Non-Deployable Service Members*, Washington, D.C.: Department of Defense, July 30, 2018. As of August 31, 2018:
http://www.esd.whs.mil/Portals/54/Documents/DD/issuances/dodi/133245p.pdf?ver=2018-08-01 -080044-667

Department of Defense Office of Financial Readiness, *A Guide to the Uniformed Services Blended Retirement System*, December 2017. As of July 9, 2018:
https://militarypay.defense.gov/Portals/3/Documents/BlendedRetirementDocuments/A%20Guide %20to%20the%20Uniformed%20Services%20BRS%20December%202017.pdf?ver=2017-12-18 -140805-343

Department of Defense Office of the Actuary, *Statistical Report on the Military Retirement System, Fiscal Year 2016*, Alexandria, Va.: Department of Defense Office of the Actuary, July 2017. As of July 2, 2018:
https://actuary.defense.gov/Portals/15/Documents/MRS_StatRpt_2016%20v4%20FINAL.pdf?ver= 2017-07-31-104724-430

DoDI—*See* Department of Defense Instruction.

DoD Office of Financial Readiness—*See* Department of Defense Office of Financial Readiness.

DoD Office of the Actuary—*See* Department of Defense Office of the Actuary.

Freedberg, Sydney J., "Stop Wasting Infantry's Time: Mattis Task Force," *Breaking Defense*, April 13, 2018. As of July 2, 2018:
https://breakingdefense.com/2018/04/stop-wasting-infantrys-time-mattis-task-force/

Garza, Raul, *United States Marine Corps Career Designation Board: Significant Factors in Predicting Selection*, thesis, Monterey, Calif.: Naval Postgraduate School, 2014. As of July 2, 2018:
https://calhoun.nps.edu/bitstream/handle/10945/41381/14Mar_Garza_Raul.pdf?sequence=1& isAllowed=y

Hosek, James, Beth J. Asch, and Michael G. Mattock, *Should the Increase in Military Pay Be Slowed?*, Santa Monica, Calif.: RAND Corporation, TR-1185-OSD, 2012. As of January 9, 2019:
https://www.rand.org/pubs/technical_reports/TR1185.html

Kamarck, Kristy N., Harry J. Thie, Marisa Adelson, and Heather Krull, *Evaluating Navy's Funded Graduate Education Program: A Return-on-Investment Framework*, Santa Monica, Calif.: RAND Corporation, MG-995-NAVY, 2010. As of January 9, 2019:
https://www.rand.org/pubs/monographs/MG995.html

Kane, Tim, *Total Volunteer Force: Lessons from the US Military on Leadership Culture and Talent Management*, Stanford, Calif.: Hoover Institution Press, 2017.

Marine Corps Order (MCO) P1900.16F, *Marine Corps Separation and Retirement Manual (MARCORSEPMAN)*, Change 2, Washington, D.C.: Department of the Navy, June 6, 2007. As of January 18, 2019:
http://dd214.us/reference/MARCORSEPMAN.pdf

Markel, M. Wade, Henry A. Leonard, Charlotte Lynch, Christina Panis, Peter Schirmer, and Carra S. Sims, *Developing U.S. Army Officers' Capabilities for Joint, Interagency, Intergovernmental, and Multinational Environments*, Santa Monica, Calif.: RAND Corporation, MG-990-A, 2011. As of January 9, 2019:
https://www.rand.org/pubs/monographs/MG990.html

Mattis, James, Memorandum for Secretaries of the Military Departments, Chairman of the Joint Chiefs of Staff, "Establishment of the Secretary of Defense Close Combat Lethality Task Force," February 8, 2018.

Moon Cronk, Terri, "Mattis: New Policy Cracks Down on Force Deployability," *U.S. Department of Defense*, February 18, 2018. As of July 2, 2018:
https://www.defense.gov/News/Article/Article/1444961/mattis-new-policy-cracks-down-on-force
-deployability/

Navy Personnel Command, *Sailor 2025*, pamphlet, December 2017. As of July 19, 2018:
http://www.public.navy.mil/bupers-npc/career/talentmanagement/Documents/Sailor2025Glossy.pdf

Parcell, Ann D., and Amanda Kraus, *Recommendations from the CNGR Implementation Plan: Exploring the Requirements of DOPMA and ROPMA*, Arlington, VA: Center for Naval Analyses, CRM D0021641.A2, 2010.

Paul, Christopher, Isaac R. Porche III, and Elliot Axelband, *The Other Quiet Professionals: Lessons for Future Cyber Forces from the Evolution of Special Forces*, Santa Monica, Calif.: RAND Corporation, RR-780-A, 2014. As of January 9, 2019:
https://www.rand.org/pubs/research_reports/RR780.html

Robbert, Albert A., Brent R. Keltner, Kenneth Reynolds, Mark Spranca, and Bernadette Benjamin, *Differentiation in Military Human Resource Management*, Santa Monica, Calif.: RAND Corporation, MR-838-OSD, 1997. As of February 7, 2018:
https://www.rand.org/pubs/monograph_reports/MR838.html

Rosen, Stephen Peter, *Winning the Next War: Innovation and the Modern Military*, Ithaca, N.Y.: Cornell University Press, 1991.

Rostker, Bernard, *Reforming the American Officer Personnel System: Addendum: Thoughts on Contractors*, Santa Monica, Calif.: RAND Corporation, CT-446/1, 2015. As of January 9, 2019:
https://www.rand.org/pubs/testimonies/CT446z1.html

Rostker, Bernard, Harry J. Thie, James L. Lacy, Jennifer H. Kawata, and Susanna W. Purnell, *The Defense Officer Personnel Management Act of 1980: A Retrospective Assessment*, Santa Monica, Calif.: RAND Corporation, R-4246-FMP, 1993. As of February 6, 2018:
https://www.rand.org/pubs/reports/R4246.html

Schirmer, Peter, Dina G. Levy, Harry J. Thie, Joy S. Moini, Margaret C. Harrell, Kimberly Curry Hall, Kevin Brancato, and Megan Abbott, *New Paths to Success: Determining Career Alternatives for Field-Grade Officers*, Santa Monica, Calif.: RAND Corporation, MG-117-OSD, 2004. As of February 16, 2018:
https://www.rand.org/pubs/monographs/MG117.html

Schirmer, Peter, Harry J. Thie, Margaret C. Harrell, and Michael S. Tseng, *Challenging Time in DOPMA: Flexible and Contemporary Military Officer Management*, Santa Monica, Calif.: RAND Corporation, MG-451-OSD, 2006. As of February 6, 2018: https://www.rand.org/pubs/monographs/MG451.html

Secretary of the Navy Instruction 1420.1B, *Promotion, Special Selection, Selective Early Retirement, and Selective Early Removal Boards for Commissioned Officers of the Navy and Marine Corps*, Washington, D.C.: Department of the Navy, March 28, 2006. As of January 18, 2019: https://doni.documentservices.dla.mil/Directives/01000%20Military%20Personnel%20Support/01 -400%20Promotion%20and%20Advancement%20Programs/1420.1B.pdf

Simons, Anna, *21st-Century Challenges of Command: A View from the Field*, Carlisle Barracks, Pa.: U.S. Army War College Press, 2017. As of June 25, 2018: https://ssi.armywarcollege.edu/pubs/display.cfm?pubID=1353

Snodgrass, Guy, and Ben Kohlmann, *2014 Navy Retention Study: 2014 Survey Report*, September 1, 2014. As of July 2, 2018: https://static1.squarespace.com/static/5353c5e1e4b073dfbc7e1326/t/5403d33fe4b0e9cf18a45ee5 /1409536831840/2014+Navy+Retention+Study+Report+-+Full.pdf

Spain, Everett Stuart Palmer, *Finding and Keeping Stars: The Leadership Performance and Retention of High-Potentials*, dissertation, Harvard University, 2014, ProQuest Dissertations Publishing, 2014.

Thie, Harry J., Margaret C. Harrell, Kevin Brancato, Jefferson P. Marquis, Clifford M. Graf II, Roland J. Yardley, and Jerry Sollinger, *Aft and Fore: A Retrospective and Prospective Analysis of Navy Officer Management*, Santa Monica, Calif.: RAND Corporation, MR-1479-NAVY, 2003. As of February 6, 2018: https://www.rand.org/pubs/monograph_reports/MR1479.html

Thie, Harry J., Margaret C. Harrell, Roger Allen Brown, Clifford M. Graf II, Mark Berends, Claire M. Levy, and Jerry Sollinger, *A Future Officer Career Management System: An Objectives-Based Design*, Santa Monica, Calif.: RAND Corporation, MR-788-OSD, 2001. As of February 16, 2018: https://www.rand.org/pubs/monograph_reports/MR788.html

U.S. Army Office of Economic and Manpower Analysis, "Talent Management," 2016. As of July 19, 2018: https://talent.army.mil/

Wilkie, Robert, Under Secretary of Defense for Personnel and Readiness, "DOD Retention Policy for Non-Deployable Service Members," memorandum for the secretaries of the Military departments, the chairman of the Joint Chiefs of Staff, the undersecretaries of defense, the deputy chief management officer, the chief of the National Guard Bureau, and the director of cost assessment and program evaluation, February 14, 2018. As of July 2, 2018: https://dod.defense.gov/Portals/1/Documents/pubs/DoD-Universal-Retention-Policy.pdf

Yardley, Roland J., Peter Schirmer, Harry J. Thie, and Samantha J. Merck, *OPNAV N14 Quick Reference: Officer Manpower and Personnel Governance in the U.S. Navy—Law, Policy, Practice*, Santa Monica, Calif.: RAND Corporation, TR-264-NAVY, 2005. As of May 25, 2018: https://www.rand.org/pubs/technical_reports/TR264.html